P9-DGP-912

PRAISE FOR

THE MEASURE OF A YOUNG MAN

For years, Gene Getz has been one of the leading voices in men's ministry. This book is truly a new classic on guiding young men toward spiritual maturity. I recommend it for every man who wants all that God has in store for him.

JIM BURNS, PH.D.
President of HomeWord
Author of *Confident Parenting* and *Teenology: The Art of Raising Great Teenagers*

Parents will discover that this powerful book contains an intensely biblical and practical blueprint for challenging their sons to rise above the smog of our society and make a spiritual impact on a calloused world. It is God's agenda for living in God's will.

DR. HOWARD HENDRICKS
Distinguished Professor Emeritus, Center for Christian Leadership
Dallas Theological Seminary

As the father of three grown sons, I heartily recommend Gene and Kenton Getz's *The Measure of a Young Man*. This is the answer to a plethora of self-help books and thin-soup lists of easy steps to raise boys in a troubling age. As a friend, colleague and beneficiary of Dr. Getz's mentoring, it didn't surprise me to find a singleminded focus on Scripture. And with the capable input of his own son, Gene has produced another masterpiece that parents and young men will find invaluable.

JERRY B. JENKINS
Owner, Christian Writers Guild and Jenkins Entertainment

Become the Man
God Wants You to Be

THE
MEASURE
OF A
YOUNG
MAN

Gene A. Getz
Bestselling Author of *The Measure of a Man*

Kenton Getz

Regal

From Gospel Light
Ventura, California, U.S.A.

Published by Regal
From Gospel Light
Ventura, California, U.S.A.
www.regalbooks.com
Printed in the U.S.A.

All Scripture quotations are taken from the *Holman Christian Standard Bible*.
© 2001, Broadman and Holman Publishers, Lifeway Christian Resources,
127 Ninth Avenue North, Nashville, TN 37234.

© 2011 Gene Getz and Kenton Getz
All rights reserved.

Library of Congress Cataloging-in-Publication Data
Getz, Gene A.
The measure of a young man / Gene Getz, Kenton Getz.
p. cm.
ISBN 978-0-8307-5759-6 (trade paper)
1. Young men—Religious life. 2. Christian men—Religious life. I. Getz, Kenton. II. Title.
BV4541.3.G48 2011
248.8'32—dc22
2011000053

Rights for publishing this book outside the U.S.A. or in non-English languages
are administered by Gospel Light Worldwide, an international not-for-profit ministry. For
additional information, please visit www.glww.org, email info@glww.org, or write to Gospel
Light Worldwide, 1957 Eastman Avenue, Ventura, CA 93003, U.S.A.

To order copies of this book and other Regal products in bulk quantities,
please contact us at 1-800-446-7735.

DEDICATION

Together, my dad and I want to dedicate this book to his five grandsons and my four sons: Kyle Fackler, Corbin Getz, Caleb Getz, Carter Getz and Cooper Getz. May God continue to draw your hearts to Him, and I pray that you will find a rich relationship with Him on your journey. More than a lifetime of effort can be committed to seeking God and allowing Him to develop your speech, life, love, faith and purity. No matter what you face in life, God is there, leading you. Hold on to this truth.

Second, I want to dedicate this book to my wife, Carla, who is a model to me in her pursuit of God. She is unwilling to settle for status quo in life. She lives by trusting in God and following Him and encourages and supports me through the thick and thin of life. Thank you, Sunshine, for your passion for God. I am honored to be your husband, and our children are blessed to have you as their mother. I love you.

Third, I want to dedicate this book to my dad, my co-author. I appreciate all the coaching and encouragement he gave me as we worked on this book together. Dad, Thank you for the years of relentless leadership in our family. You have never departed from your faith in God and have consistently "walked your talk!" Thank you!

Fourth, I want to dedicate this book to my mother, who is everything my dad says she is in the acknowledgements. She is not only my mother but is also a friend and our family's biggest fan. Thank you, mom, for being there and supporting Carla and me and loving our kids. Our children are privileged and fortunate to grow up knowing you. They look forward to their "Nana" days and treasure their special relationship with you, just as I have. Thanks, mom!

Finally, I want to thank my Sunday morning coffee group: Dan Martin, Greg Ligon and Greg Dudrow. Without you in my life, this book would not have been possible. I appreciate your friendship and being on life's journey with you.

Kenton Getz

Contents

UNIT 1: DISCOVER WHO YOU ARE

   To become the man God wants you to become, you must begin by receiving the Lord Jesus Christ as your personal Savior.

   Even though you are a young man, you should ask God to strengthen and encourage you so you can accomplish what may appear to be an awesome task.

   To overcome fear, you must establish your own identity by discovering who you are in Jesus Christ.

UNIT 2: BE AN EXAMPLE

   To be a good example to others, you are to imitate Christ's life.

   To develop a good reputation, you must allow God's Word to penetrate your heart and change your life as you meet with others to study the Word of God and to have Christian fellowship.

   In order to be an example to others, you must develop Christlike character traits.

UNIT 3: WATCH YOUR WORDS

UNIT 4: LIVE LIFE IN GOD'S WILL

UNIT 5: LOVE AS CHRIST LOVED

UNIT 6: DEVELOP YOUR FAITH

UNIT 7: MAINTAIN MORAL PURITY

ACKNOWLEDGMENTS

First of all, I want to acknowledge Elaine, my wife, and Kenton's mother. She has not only been a wonderful, supportive partner to me but also a devoted mom to Kenton.

I remember so well an unusual event that reflects the quality of their relationship. Between Kenton's junior and senior years at Baylor University, he had the opportunity to take an extension course in finance in London, England. He approached his mother and asked if she would be interested in joining him for couple of weeks to travel throughout Europe—hiking, staying nights in a bed and breakfast and traveling from place to place by rail. When Elaine shared Kenton's request with me, I responded with great enthusiasm, reminding her that few college age sons rarely ask their mothers to join them in this kind of adventure. Elaine responded positively to Kenton's invitation, and together they traveled to some of the great sites throughout Europe—particularly in Germany, Switzerland and Austria.

So, thanks, Elaine, for being a great mother to our son. Without your godly example as well as your verbal input in his life, we would not be writing this book together.

Second, Kenton and I want to say thank you to Josh and Sean McDowell, who graciously wrote the foreword to this book. Both of us admire their father-son ministry together.

Finally, we want to thank Sue Mitchell, my dedicated administrative assistant, who spent many hours using her excellent word processing skills and insights to help prepare this manuscript for publication.

Gene A. Getz

FOREWORD

Our friend, Gene Getz, wrote a classic book when he penned *The Measure of a Man*. And now, here's a companion book entitled *The Measure of a Young Man*—but totally new and different. It's based on Paul's challenge to Timothy: "No one should despise your youth; instead, you should be an example to the believers in speech, in conduct, in love, in faith, in purity" (1 Timothy 4:12).

When the good people at Regal asked Gene to write this new book, he asked his son, Kenton, to join him, using this basic Scripture text as the outline. In many respects, this is not a new concept for Kenton. Beginning in junior high school, Gene wrote him a series of letters based on this charge to Timothy and continued this kind of correspondence through Kenton's high school and college years.

In this book, you'll get to know Timothy—his childhood, his conversion experience, his unique relationship with Paul. You'll learn principles from this young man's life that will help you keep your eyes on Jesus Christ in your own life journey. As another father-and-son team, we highly recommend this book.

Josh D. McDowell
Sean McDowell

A Letter from Gene

Dear Young Friend,

Nearly 2,000 years ago, a young man named Timothy lived in a very pagan city called Lystra. Like most cities in the Roman world, whole families witnessed open immorality in the pagan temples. Illicit sexual activity was a part of their religious worship. But as a young single man, Timothy became a believer in the Lord Jesus Christ and distinguished himself as an example of godliness and sexual purity in a society that was far more decadent than our own today.

When the apostle Paul wrote his first letter to Timothy, he had left him in Ephesus to help Christians mature in Christ. To carry out this awesome responsibility, Paul encouraged this young man with these very challenging words:

> No one should *despise your youth*; instead, you should be an *example* to the believers in *speech*, in *conduct*, in *love*, in *faith*, in *purity* (1 Timothy 4:12, emphasis added).

In this book, *The Measure of a Young Man,* my son, Kenton, and I want to help you look carefully at this spiritual assignment that Paul gave to Timothy. You'll discover that what he wrote is applicable to your life as well. Here is what Paul challenged Timothy—and you—to do:

- Discover who you are
- Always be an example
- Watch your words
- Live life fully in God's will
- Love others as Christ loved you
- Develop your faith
- Maintain a life of moral purity

Thanks for joining us on this spiritual journey! Though we may never meet you on this earth, we look forward to seeing you someday when we all meet Jesus Christ face to face!

Gene Getz

INTRODUCTION

A Letter from Kenton

Dear Friend,

Milestones. In junior high, it was a party at a friend's house to celebrate the end of the school year. The summer before my ninth-grade year, it was an overseas missions trip to Sweden. On my sixteenth birthday, it was a driver's license and the keys to a 1972 AMC Gremlin—yellow with black racing stripes . . . a great first car. Gremlins were not made to last very long, and by the time I was done with it, the only thing left of value was the air conditioner.

After graduating from high school, it was moving into the dorm room at Baylor University to start my college years. After my sophomore year at Baylor, it was moving to Frisco, Colorado, to join the Summit County Race Team. I wanted to see how a Texan could compete in snow ski racing against kids who grew up on skis. Then, upon graduating from Baylor, I got my first job in accounting.

These events in my life are some examples of times when I was on my own and responsible for making my own decisions. Each event represented a step toward independence from my parents. Your own milestone events are important to you because you are on the same path of developing your independence. Your story is different from mine. Your circumstances are different. Times are different. But the process of growing up is a reality! It's happening to you.

The real question is, "Will you choose to become a man of God as you grow older?" This is a big question and one that I have had to face daily. This is why the words of 1 Timothy 4:12 are such an encouragement and challenge to me. This is a short, direct and powerful verse. It touches on seven areas that impact the quality of your relationships with God, your family, your friends and your future spouse.

When I went on my first missionary trip, my dad began writing me a series of letters based on this challenge to Timothy. Over the course of several years, he continued these letters—while I was counseling in a Christian camp and later while I was a competitive ski racer in Colorado. I'm thankful for these letters that challenged me to be an example in these areas:

- *Speech* (talking and communicating with others)
- *Conduct* (living daily and making choices)

- *Love* (protecting your heart and treating others well)
- *Faith* (measuring what you believe against Scripture and living your beliefs)
- *Purity* (protecting your mind and body, and protecting others)

Choose today to start the *adventure* of becoming a man of God. Work through the pages of this book and practice the applications at the end of each chapter. Paul's challenge to Timothy is God's challenge to you. He *will* shape your heart and the hearts of your friends.

Kenton Getz

UNIT 1

Discover Who You Are

No one should despise your youth.
1 TIMOTHY 4:12

One of the great challenges we all face as young men growing up is to discover who we are as individuals. We call this our *identity*. Though God has created each one of us as unique personalities, the imperfect world in which we live often impacts us in negative ways. In fact, some grown men actually go through life trying to be someone else rather than the person God intended them to be.

What you read in the next three chapters has been written to help you answer the question, "Who am I?" You will also discover three dynamic principles to live by.

1

Discovering a New Life

PRINCIPLE TO LIVE BY

To become the man God wants you to become, you must begin
by receiving the Lord Jesus Christ as your personal Savior.

Meet Timothy, a young man who grew up in the city of Lystra. The majority of the people there were pagan Gentiles who worshiped the Greek gods Zeus and Hermes. Fortunately, Timothy's mother was a God-fearing Jewish woman who taught him about the God of Abraham, Isaac and Jacob.

MIRACLES IN LYSTRA (ACTS 14:8-20)

When Paul and his missionary companion Barnabas entered Lystra, they began to share the good news regarding the gift of eternal life through faith in the Lord Jesus Christ. While Paul was explaining the salvation story, he noticed a crippled man who was listening intently and "had faith to be healed" (Acts 14:9). Consequently, Paul called out, "Stand up straight on your feet!" (v. 10). Instantly, God healed the man, and for the first time in his life, he could walk!

The crowd of people who saw what happened were amazed. They instantly thought that their god Hermes had become a man in the person of Paul. They also believed that Barnabas was Zeus, and they began to worship these missionaries.

Paul and Barnabas were shocked and mortified. They literally "tore their robes" (v. 14), shouting that they were mere men—not gods. But then something unexpected happened. Some angry Jews turned the crowd against them. They focused their hostility on Paul and stoned him. Thinking he was dead, they dumped his body outside the city.

Then another miraculous event took place. As a group of believers surrounded Paul, he supernaturally stood up, went back into the city and then he and Barnabas went on to another city. It was sometime during these events that Timothy and his mother, Eunice, heard the message of salvation and put their faith in the Lord Jesus Christ.

CHILDHOOD EXPERIENCES

Let's look more closely at Timothy's experiences as a young boy growing up in this pagan city. He had observed pagan worship that was often associated with all kinds of sexual immorality. In fact, Timothy's own father was probably a man who worshiped the Greek gods Zeus and Hermes. He may have actually witnessed or at least heard about his dad's sexual unfaithfulness to his mother. This would not be surprising, since it happened throughout the Roman Empire.

But in spite of growing up in this pagan city, Timothy's mother taught him a lot about the Old Testament. In Paul's second letter to Timothy, he reminded him that he had "known the sacred Scriptures" from the time he was just a young boy (2 Timothy 3:15).

THE MIRACLE AT MOUNT SINAI

What had Timothy's mother taught him? We, of course, can only speculate, but we certainly can conclude that she told him how God delivered the children of Israel from Egypt. More importantly, she would have taught him the Ten Commandments. Timothy would have been amazed when he heard what happened at Mount Sinai when God literally spoke from the mountain consumed with fire and smoke and then inscribed these commandments on two tablets of stone. As he saw the idolatrous activities all around him—and on a daily basis—the first two commandments would have become deeply embedded in his mind:

> Do not have other gods besides Me. Do not make an idol for yourself, whether in the shape of anything in the heavens above or on the earth below or in the waters under the earth. You must not bow down to them or worship them (Exodus 20:3-5).

Though we may not engage in idolatry like the people in the city where Timothy lived, what are some of the things in your life that can become an idol—that is, something more important than God?

AN OLD TESTAMENT ROLE MODEL

Perhaps one of Timothy's favorite stories involved Daniel. He was just a young man, 15 years old, when he and three other young men about his age were taken from their families and deported to Babylon, when Nebuchadnezzar made his first attack on Jerusalem. Once there, these teenagers were chosen to enter a Babylonian school where they were trained in all aspects of pagan religion.

Nebuchadnezzar had plans for these four young men, and he insisted that they eat the best food and drink the best wine in his kingdom. However, Daniel "determined that he would not defile himself with the king's food or with the wine he drank" (Daniel 1:8a). He actually made this decision in his heart. He knew this food and drink had already been offered to pagan gods, and he did not want to acknowledge these false deities and honor them in any way. Consequently, he asked permission from the chief official not to defile himself (see Daniel 1:8b).

God honored Daniel's decision, and his three friends joined him in making this commitment. They could have lost their lives for refusing to obey the king, but they prospered physically and intellectually, and later graduated with honors (see Daniel 1:8-21). As a result of their determination to honor God in these difficult circumstances, Daniel and his three friends became bold witnesses for the Lord in this pagan culture for years to come.

Daniel's story would have prepared Timothy for his own bold decision to put his faith in Jesus Christ. Paul referred to that decision in his second letter to Timothy when he wrote:

> And that from childhood you have known the sacred Scriptures, which are able to instruct you for salvation through faith in Christ Jesus (2 Timothy 3:15).

PRINCIPLE TO LIVE BY
RECEIVING CHRIST

To become the man God wants you to become, you must begin by receiving the Lord Jesus Christ as your personal Savior.

WHAT ABOUT YOU?

We don't know your family background. We know nothing about your friends. Maybe both of your parents are Christians. Like Timothy's parents, maybe one of your parents follows Christ and the other one doesn't. Maybe your parents are divorced. Maybe there are no Christians in your family at all. Maybe your parents claim to be Christians but they don't live like it—and that kind of hypocrisy has left a bad taste in your mouth!

Regardless of our backgrounds, we all have a problem that keeps us from God, and that problem is "sin." When you realize that you are a sinner, you are at a point of decision. You can either turn to Jesus and accept Him as your Savior, or you can reject what Jesus has done for you and go on living for yourself.

When I (Kenton) was five years old, I heard the story of Jesus and that He died and rose from the grave as a sacrifice for the whole world's sins. When I got home from school, I talked to my mother about the story of Jesus. She helped me understand that I wasn't perfect and that I had sinned. This sin in my life was going to keep me out of heaven unless I accepted God's gift and invited Jesus into my life. She prayed with me that day. I knew I was a sinner and that Jesus did a wonderful thing by dying for me and taking my penalty. I turned to Jesus and thanked Him, and then invited Him into my heart.

God has that same gift for you, but it's a decision only you can make! First, you must *recognize and acknowledge that you are a sinner and need a Savior!* You see, not one of us is perfect. There is no one without some sin. We are not like God, who is completely holy. Consequently, we fall short of measuring up to His glory. Furthermore, the Bible states that the result of our sins is spiritual death and separation from God. Consider the following verses from Paul's letter to the Romans:

For all have sinned and fall short of the glory of God (Romans 3:23).

For the wages of sin is death, but the gift of God is eternal life in Christ Jesus our Lord (Romans 6:23).

Second, you must believe and confess that Jesus Christ died for your sins and rose again. At the same time, you need to ask the Lord to save you, and He will respond to your prayer. Consider the following response when the jailor in Philippi asked Paul and Silas how he could be saved:

Then he escorted them out and said, "Sirs, what must I do to be saved?" So they said, "Believe on the Lord Jesus, and you will be saved—you and your household" (Acts 16:30-31).

A SIMPLE PRAYER

To help you turn to Jesus, here is a suggested prayer. Pray these words sincerely and, like Timothy, you will have a life-changing experience that will continue until God calls you home to heaven:

Dear Jesus, I confess that I'm a sinner and I need a Savior. I believe that You are the Son of God and that You took the punishment for my sins and died in my place. I believe that God raised You from the dead and You are alive today. I open the door to my heart and ask You to come in and be the Lord of my life. Thank You, Jesus, for loving me and accepting me as I am. Thank You for coming into my life and saving me. In Jesus' name, amen.

Now that you have prayed this prayer, read it one more time and sign your name and place the date in the space provided. If you had already made this decision, sign your name now, and if you can, record the date when you received the Lord Jesus Christ as your personal Savior.*

Name _____

Date _____

A FINAL CHALLENGE

If you prayed this prayer, be sure to share your experience with another Christian who can encourage you and help you grow in your Christian life.

---

* **Note:** The fact that you cannot pinpoint the exact time and date when you received the Lord Jesus Christ as your Savior does not necessarily mean that you are not saved. The important thing is that you know that you have believed in Christ and that He is your Savior. However, if you are uncertain of your salvation, you can make sure today by sincerely praying the above prayer and signing the form and including the date.

2

Praying for Courage

Even though you are a young man, you should ask God to strengthen and encourage you so you can accomplish what may appear to be an awesome task.

When Paul returned to Lystra several years later, on his second missionary journey, he had a wonderful surprise. He heard about Timothy's decision to follow Christ. Even Christians from a neighboring city were talking about this young man's commitment to living in God's will. Luke reported in the book of Acts that "the brothers at Lystra and Iconium spoke highly of him" (Acts 16:2).

Though there were certainly many conversations that took place between Paul and Timothy's family that we know nothing about, one thing is certain: Paul was impressed with Timothy and wanted this young man to join him as his missionary companion.

It must have been difficult for Timothy's mother, Eunice, to allow her son to leave home and join Paul on a journey that would be very difficult and even dangerous. After all, she had seen angry people attempt to kill Paul several years before. However, she certainly gave her permission and trusted God to protect her son. In fact, in Paul's second letter to Timothy, he commended Eunice for her "sincere faith" (2 Timothy 1:5).

Regarding Timothy's father—who was not a believer—there must have been no resistance. Perhaps he just didn't care! In fact, he may never have become a believer in Jesus Christ.

As far as we can tell, Timothy was at Paul's side for a number of years. He became a faithful and dedicated servant of Christ; and when Paul was released from his first imprisonment, he then entrusted Timothy with an enormous responsibility—to help resolve some very difficult problems in the church in Ephesus.

AN AWESOME TASK!

Imagine, if you can, what it would be like to be in Timothy's shoes. Men older than he was—some by many years—were not teaching the truth. They were creating arguments in the church, and Paul told Timothy to "command" these men to stop acting this way (see 1 Timothy 1:3-4)!

This *was* an awesome task. Understandably, Timothy was anxious and fearful. Some of these men would reject him and even accuse him of being arrogant. Others were living such sinful lives that they might even try to harm him. To make it even scarier for Timothy, he faced men who wanted to become official pastors but who were not spiritually qualified (see 1 Timothy 3:1,8; 5:17,19).

Most of these men had families of their own, and Timothy was still young and single. If you had his assignment, how would you respond to crusty old men who got in your face, literally shouting, "Who are you to evaluate us as prospective spiritual leaders? You're just a kid, and you don't even have children of your own!"

How would you feel if you were responsible to lead men older than you were, even if they were spiritually mature?

Timothy faced even bigger problems. Some of the men who were already official leaders were engaging in sinful and selfish behavior. Understandably, Timothy needed Paul's encouragement. This is why Paul wrote, "No one should despise your youth" (1 Timothy 4:12a). In other words, "Don't let anyone look down on you, Timothy, because you're a young man! Don't allow fear and intimidation to keep you from carrying out your tasks—as difficult as they are!"

AN OLD TESTAMENT EXAMPLE

Having heard Old Testament stories from the time he was just a boy, Timothy certainly remembered Joshua's experience (see 2 Timothy 3:15). Even as an older man, Joshua faced the awesome task of leading the children of Israel into the Promised Land. The parents of the younger generation had all died in the wilderness because of their sinful disobedience. Even Moses had difficulty leading them to live in God's will. Would this new generation act any differently?

Joshua's fears were understandable. He was actually trembling. Consequently, the Lord spoke to him and repeatedly challenged him to "be strong and courageous" (Joshua 1:6-7,9). Paul issued the same challenge to young Timothy. And he is saying the same thing to you! When you're discouraged, depressed and fearful, "be strong and courageous!" But most importantly, remember God's promise that He will always be with you!

PRINCIPLE TO LIVE BY
PRAY FOR COURAGE
——————

Even though you are a young man, you should ask God to strengthen and encourage you so you can accomplish what may appear to be an awesome task.

My father, Gene Getz, has devoted his life to studying the Bible. God has given him opportunities to minister to people all over the world and to teach them biblical principles. When he studies the Scriptures, he looks at what God is saying in a particular passage and then finds other chapters and verses where God is communicating the same truth. The truths that emerge from these passages can also be called "principles to live by."

When we look at the Bible as a whole, we can see that God has related to His followers in a consistent way for thousands of years. God uses the biblical stories of people's lives to communicate principles by which we should live. If correctly stated, these principles never change. They are applicable as long as we live on this earth, and they will guide us on our adventure of becoming men of God.

For example, this second principle that emerges from our study of 1 Timothy 4:12 relates to Paul's opening statement to Timothy: "No one should despise your youth." Even if people try to discourage you, God wants to use you in special ways, even though you are young. Your tasks will certainly never be as awesome as Timothy's, but your fears and anxieties may be similar. In spite of your feelings, we want to encourage you to let God use you.

PRAYING SPECIFICALLY

In view of this principle, we want you to take one significant step. Simply ask God to show you what special task He may have for you at this very moment in your life. Perhaps you already know what this task is. If so, ask God for courage to tackle it in His strength. Here are some examples for prayer:

- Pray for courage to share the message about Christ with a friend, a family member, a boss or teacher.
- Pray for courage to talk with a friend who is making decisions that are out of alignment with God's will.
- Pray for courage to lovingly confront a bully who keeps picking on boys younger than he is.

- Pray for courage to teach a Sunday School class of younger kids.
- Pray for courage to apply for a particular job.
- Pray for courage to try out for a particular sport.
- Pray for courage to ask an older godly person to mentor you.
- Other _____

PRAYER PROMISES

Before you pray specifically, meditate on the following promise from the Bible:

Don't worry about anything, but in everything, through prayer and petition with thanksgiving, let your requests be made known to God. And the peace of God, which surpasses every thought, will guard your hearts and your minds in Christ Jesus (Philippians 4:6-7).

PRAYER PARTNERS

To carry out this step, we encourage you to ask a close friend to join you in prayer as you seek God's will. Remember that Jesus said:

Again, I assure you: If two of you on earth agree about any matter that you pray for, it will be done for you by My Father in heaven. For where two or three are gathered in My name, I am there among them (Matthew 18:19-20).

3

Overcoming Fear

PRINCIPLE TO LIVE BY

To overcome fear, you must establish your own identity
by discovering who you are in Jesus Christ.

We all experience fear. It's a God-created emotion. Without it we would all be in trouble. Fear keeps us from doing stupid things. On the other hand, if you constantly experience fear that is so intense it keeps you from leaving your house or making friends or doing your job, you're also in serious trouble. God does not want you to live with this kind of anxiety and worry.

Timothy struggled with fear that at times made him hesitant to do what God wanted him to do. His mentor, the apostle Paul, understood this tendency in his young friend. That's why, in his final letter, he wrote to Timothy and encouraged him with these very direct words:

> For God has not given us a *spirit of fearfulness*, but one of power, love, and sound judgment (2 Timothy 1:7, emphasis added).

Why did Timothy struggle with fear? Here are some predictable and understandable reasons. Perhaps you can identify in some ways with his experience.

AN UNSAVED FATHER

We're never told how Timothy's father responded when his wife and son became Christians. It appears that he may have rejected the message of salvation for years to come. In other words, Timothy grew up in a home where he only had one parent—his mother—who believed in Jesus.

This was not an ideal home background, just as Timothy's overall environment was not ideal. In fact, the world around him was permeated with idolatry and immorality. And even though he had a godly mother, not having a strong Christian father certainly impacted him in negative ways. Though later in life he had a wonderful father substitute in the apostle

Paul, no one can totally make up for a father who is not a good example to his son in his early years. Perhaps this is one reason why Timothy at times became intensely fearful and anxious.

A THREATENING ENVIRONMENT

The apostle Paul also understood Timothy's tendency to become anxious and intimidated because of persecution. As a young man, he was probably standing among those disciples who saw Paul stoned in his hometown and who gathered around Paul when he was left for dead (see Acts 14:19-20). Even though God miraculously enabled Paul to survive this terrible experience, we can be sure that Timothy never forgot that horrible scene.

Although your experiences are certainly far different than Timothy's, what has caused lingering fears in your life?

What happened in Timothy's hometown was just the beginning of persecution for Paul and his missionary team. How could this young man ever forget what happened in Philippi when he saw both Paul and Silas beaten with rods and inflicted with many blows, and then locked up in the inner prison with hardened criminals (see Acts 16:22-24)? And once again, even though Paul, his spiritual father, along with Silas were miraculously delivered, how could he ever forget that incredible night? Paul understood Timothy's lingering fear and often encouraged his young companion.

PRINCIPLE TO LIVE BY
YOUR IDENTITY IN CHRIST

**To overcome fear, you must establish your own identity
by discovering who you are in Jesus Christ.**

A SCARY EXPERIENCE

Growing up, I (Kenton) was the youngest in our family. I have two older sisters who are six and seven years older than me. So, when I was in early elementary school, they were starting their teenage years. Needless to say, they watched some things on TV that scared me to death and had a profound impact on my fear of the dark.

That fear relates to a movie I saw on TV involving a mother who was at home with her baby and the housekeeper. A terrible storm was raging outside. She lost the power to her home. Her husband was going to be delayed because of a problem on the highway.

The next thing I saw was the woman telling the housekeeper that everything was going to be okay. She could leave and go home. The scene then moved to the front of the house and showed the housekeeper getting into her car. The camera then shifted to a window on the second story where the woman was frantically pounding on the glass and yelling at the housekeeper, trying to get her attention to stay.

In the next scene, a bolt of lightning lit up the house, and the woman came face to face with her double, who had an evil scowl on her face and laughed an evil laugh. The double pointed her finger at the woman and said in a terrible and hideous voice, "I want your baby."

The woman ran to the baby's room and slammed the door and locked it. The camera then zoomed in on the deadbolt and showed it mysteriously turning very slowly. The door opened and you could see two shadows, the woman in a corner of the room holding her baby and the evil double walking toward her. The woman was grasping her baby and screaming. The double was laughing an evil laugh, and then she grabbed the woman by the neck and began to choke her, screaming, "I want your baby!"

Just then, the husband arrived home. He ran into the house and up the stairs and found his wife alive, holding the baby, and crying. The evil double had disappeared and was nowhere to be seen. The show was over—but not my memory of what happened.

So what was the impact of this movie on a young kid? I did not want to sleep in my room for fear that something bad was going to happen to me. Also, the next time we had a storm and the lights went out, I wouldn't leave my mother's side because who knows what I would find in our house in the dark. To this day, when the lights go out in a storm, I have memories of that movie, and I can recall the scenes and the characters in my mind's eye.

FEAR . . . OVERCOMING NEGATIVE EXPERIENCES

The brain is a powerful organ, and it is a gift from God. It's like a computer. It records everything that you take in and stores all of your memories. It draws upon your past experiences and forms a foundational grid for how you make decisions. This is why it's important to fill your mind with thoughts and truths that are edifying, and not destructive.

You are in a constant battle with the world system, which is working to program your mind and win your thoughts for its own purposes. Just like you have to protect your computer from harmful programs designed to take over your computer, you must also protect your mind. The world is full of viruses, worms, and phishing tactics designed to sidetrack you from the truth of who you are in Christ. The author of the world system that tries to distract you from pursuing God is described in the Bible as a very real threat to your life. In 1 Peter 5:8, Satan is described as a "roaring lion":

> Be sober! Be on the alert! *Your adversary the Devil* is prowling around *like a roaring lion*, looking for anyone he can devour (emphasis added).

Fear is one of Satan's strongest tactics! He used it on Timothy most of his life. But Satan was not victorious. In spite of Timothy's tendencies to be gripped by this negative emotion, he knew who he was in Jesus Christ. He had a new identity. This is what Paul meant when he wrote to the Corinthians:

> Therefore if anyone is in Christ, there is a new creation; old things have passed away, and look, new things have come (2 Corinthians 5:17).

WHO YOU ARE IN CHRIST

Whenever you experience fear, think of your identity with and in Christ. Here are some wonderful scriptural truths to think about. Check (√) those that might help you the most to overcome fear and anxiety:

- ❑ I am God's child (John 1:12; 1 John 3:1-3).
- ❑ I have been redeemed and forgiven of all my sins (Colossians 1:14).
- ❑ I have been adopted as God's child (Ephesians 1:5).
- ❑ I am in God's family (Ephesians 2:19).
- ❑ I am Christ's friend (John 15:15).
- ❑ I cannot be separated from God's love (Romans 8:35).
- ❑ I have the Holy Spirit living in me (Ephesians 1:13-14).
- ❑ I can do all things through Christ who strengthens me (Philippians 4:13).
- ❑ Since I am born of God, Satan cannot touch me (1 John 5:18).

A FATHER'S REFLECTION

When Kenton penned this story, it was the first time I had heard it. Had I known why he was so fearful, what could I, as his father, have done differently to help him overcome it? How could I have encouraged him to be open with me as a young son? In fact, why didn't he share this story with me? Perhaps he tried, but I missed what he was trying to say.

If you have "fears" that continue to bother you, talk to your dad or mom or another understanding adult. You might share Kenton's story, even though "your fears" are related to a totally different situation.

UNIT 2

Be an Example

*No one should despise your youth; instead,
you should be an example to the believers...*
1 TIMOTHY 4:12

When Paul wrote his letters to Timothy, he challenged this young man to always be an example to others. Since we all need to hear the Word of God, Timothy was "to proclaim the message" of the Bible (2 Timothy 4:2). However, he was also to demonstrate with his life how a Christian is supposed to live. In fact, this is what made his "words" meaningful to others.

How have godly examples impacted your life, and what kind of example are you to others? The following three chapters will help you answer these questions as you discover principles to live by.

4

Walking Your Talk

To be a good example to others, you are to imitate Christ's life.

As a very young professor at Moody Bible Institute, I (Gene) distinctly remember sitting in chapel one day, listening to our president. I was only 23 years old and teaching students older than I was. Dr. Culbertson was speaking to the students as well as the faculty. He looked first at the students and said, "Young people, you will forget what your teachers say." He then looked at us and finished his thought: "But you'll never forget who they are!"

I've never forgotten that moment—and that message. The president's words penetrated my mind and heart. I realized as never before how important it is to be an *example* to those we are teaching.

Perhaps you can identify with this experience. Even in your short life you have had a lot of teachers. Think for a moment about what you've learned from what they have taught you with words. Now think about what you remember about how they lived.

A TIME OF DOUBT

I remember another experience that dramatically impacted my life as a young man. While in college, I was helping out a church and became very disillusioned because several Christian leaders were living inconsistent lives. I became so confused that I began to question most everything I had been taught about Christianity.

I went through a very dark period in my life. However, I eventually refocused my thoughts and emotions, realizing that I needed to once again keep my eyes on the Lord Jesus Christ who was and is the only Person who will never let me down.

But going through this difficult time taught me another powerful spiritual lesson. Though all of us should realize that only the Lord Jesus Christ is the same yesterday, today and forever, it's God's will that others be able to look at us as godly examples. Even though we will never live perfect lives on this earth, we are to live consistent lives and be able to say by example what Paul wrote about himself: "Be imitators of me, as I also am of Christ" (1 Corinthians 11:1).

PAUL'S EXAMPLE

Timothy already understood how important modeling the message of Christ is when he was explaining God's Word to others. However, he learned this principle not so much from what Paul said, but from how his mentor lived. Again and again he had observed Paul's Christlike lifestyle. For example, when Paul wrote a letter to the Christians in Thessalonica, he commented on how he and Silas and Timothy had lived among these new converts:

> You are witnesses, and so is God, of how *devoutly, righteously,* and *blamelessly* we conducted ourselves with you believers (1 Thessalonians 2:10, emphasis added).

This is just one church-planting event that taught Timothy how important modeling the message of Christ is in effectively communicating this message with "words." He had witnessed firsthand how Paul lived among people when he was teaching biblical truth. He not only proclaimed God's Word, but he also exemplified it in his life. He lived what he taught.

In what ways can you "walk your talk" more consistently?

> ## A PRINCIPLE TO LIVE BY
> ## MODELING CHRIST
>
> **To be a good example to others, you are to imitate Christ's life.**

Think for a moment how this applies to you and me. How many of us could actually encourage others to follow our example as we follow Christ's example? In fact, this is a sobering thought for both of us as Kenton and I write these words to you. Though you may never get to know us personally and observe up close whether or not we "practice what we preach," there will be those who will—especially our wives, our children and our grandchildren. This message to you is also a message to us!

SURPRISE, SURPRISE . . .

I (Kenton) want to clear the decks and be totally honest. Ready? I am not perfect. I make mistakes. There are days where I make decisions based on my own selfish desires. There are times when you could point at my life and say, "You aren't walking your talk!"

At times my *speech* doesn't edify! I say something that tears someone down instead of building him up. My *conduct* can be prideful! I think I am right about something and come across as arrogant and unwilling to listen to others. When that happens, my attitude is *unloving*. I ignore the needs and desires of others and serve myself, and my own goals.

Paul also told Timothy to be an "example . . . in faith" and "in purity." At times, my *faith* in God suffers. I get anxious and fearful about something and work to gain control of the situation instead of trusting God. And, as with most men, I struggle with *purity* and keeping my thought life in check. For example, watching TV is a battleground. I must be careful of the television shows that I watch. Many programs on basic cable contain sensual scenes with attractive women that plant visual images in my mind. These images often give rise to lustful thoughts, and those thoughts must be fought and taken captive.

Struggling with our own selfish desires is nothing new. As a matter of fact, even Paul struggled with wanting to do the "right" thing, but finding himself doing the "wrong" thing. Paul describes this battle in his letter to the Romans:

> For I do not understand what I am doing, because I do not practice what I want to do, but I do what I hate (Romans 7:15).

Like me, I'm sure that you want to do good, but at times you find yourself doing the opposite. Maybe you have positive periods in your life, but then you suddenly struggle with selfishness. Old sinful patterns creep back into your life or new sinful patterns develop. You find yourself back in the war of wanting to do good but doing just the opposite. Are you surprised when this happens? I know that I am surprised; but we shouldn't be, because Paul experienced the same struggle. He never gave up hope.

WALKING THE TALK WHEN YOU WOULD RATHER DO THE OPPOSITE

What do we do when we struggle with temptation and sinful behavior? Paul gives an answer in the same passage:

What a wretched man I am! *Who will rescue me from this body of death?*
I thank God through Jesus Christ our Lord (Romans 7:24-25a, emphasis added)!

The mere existence of our selfish desires points to our need for Jesus.
Paul understood the battle, and he saw no hope of solving it on his own.
Consequently, he went on to give an answer to this human dilemma:

I thank God through Jesus Christ our Lord! . . . Therefore, no con-
demnation now exists for those in Christ Jesus, because *the*
Spirit's law of life in Christ Jesus has set you free from the law of sin and of
death (Romans 7:25a; 8:1-2, emphasis added).

If you have received the Lord Jesus Christ as your personal Savior, you
can "walk your talk" because Jesus has delivered you from this trap. But
don't be surprised and feel like a failure when you struggle or even fail.
The foundation to "walking your talk" is your faith in Jesus and knowing
that He delivered you from a dilemma that you could not solve. Our efforts alone can never solve the problem. When we allow the Holy Spirit to
guide us and empower us—moment by moment and day by day—we can
live in God's will.

DAD'S SURPRISE QUESTION

I distinctly remember a conversation I had with my dad one day as we were
driving from Waco, Texas. I was a student at Baylor. Out of the blue, he
asked me why I had not become a rebellious teenager. I was surprised at his
question. You see, I had done some things I was ashamed of—some of which
Dad didn't know anything about. But it was also true that I had not become a "prodigal son." I could have certainly reflected more Christlike behavior, but I knew my faith in Christ was real.

I remember my response. "Dad," I said, "it's simple. You and Mom walk
your talk!" I quickly added that I knew they were not perfect. They make
mistakes! But overall they lived consistent lives. They "walked their talk"—
which impacted my own life.

A SPECIAL ASSIGNMENT

For a wonderful Old Testament study, meditate on Psalm 1. First, notice
the progression in verse 1 that leads to sinful behavior. Underscore the
words that describe this progression:

How happy is the man who does not follow the advice of the wicked, or take the path of sinners, or join a group of mockers!

Second, notice the contrast in verse 2. Underscore the words that describe this contrast:

Instead, his delight is in the LORD's instruction, and he meditates on it day and night

Third, notice the illustration of a tree in verse 3. Underscore the words that describe our lives when we focus on living in God's will.

He is like a tree planted beside streams of water that bears its fruit in season and whose leaf does not wither. Whatever he does prospers.

A PERSONAL APPLICATION

In view of these verses, what goals would you like to set for your life?

5

Building a Good Reputation

PRINCIPLE TO LIVE BY

To develop a good reputation, you must allow God's Word to penetrate your heart and change your life as you meet with others to study the Word of God and to have Christian fellowship.

Think about the guys you know in your neighborhood, your school and your church. Who comes to mind when you think about the guys with a good reputation? What about those with a bad reputation? Why is this true? In other words, what characteristics create a good reputation and what characteristics create a bad one?

Before you read further, make a list of the actions that create a good reputation and a list of the actions that create a bad reputation.

Actions that create a good reputation	Actions that create a bad reputation

ABOVE REPROACH

When Paul wrote to Timothy, he outlined a maturity profile for selecting spiritual leaders. This list of character qualities actually describes what Christian maturity looks like for all Christians (see 1 Timothy 3:1-13).

At the top of the list is being "above reproach" (1 Timothy 3:2). This simply means having a good reputation. It's not about being perfect. Remember, there is only one man who lived a perfect life on this earth. Most of you know who that is—the Lord Jesus Christ.

This was possible because He was and is the "God-man." This simply means that when Jesus came and walked on planet Earth, He was God in human flesh. He lived a sinless life so that He could be the perfect sacrifice for our sins. John the Baptist called Jesus "the Lamb of God, who takes away the sin of the world!" (John 1:29).

POSITIVE FEEDBACK

Timothy had developed a good reputation even before he became a missionary. When Paul returned to Timothy's hometown several years after this young man had become a believer, Luke recorded that "the brothers at Lystra and Iconium *spoke highly of him*" (Acts 16:2, emphasis added).

From this brief statement we can learn three things about Timothy's reputation:

1. People were talking about this young man in a very positive way. They "spoke *highly of him*" (Acts 16:2c, emphasis added).

2. There was more than one person talking about Timothy's good reputation. "The *brothers* . . . spoke highly of him" (Acts 16:2a, emphasis added).

3. People were talking about Timothy's reputation in more than one location. "The brothers at *Lystra* and *Iconium* spoke highly of him" (Acts 16:2b, emphasis added).

This is a good test for all of us in determining whether or not we are developing a good reputation. There will be positive conversations about us among a variety of people in various locations—at home and away from home.

When people look at the way you live, what would you like for them to say?

"TRAINING IN RIGHTEOUSNESS"

When Timothy became a Christian, he began to grow spiritually. The very "sacred Scriptures" that he had learned "from childhood" and that enabled him to become a believer helped him imitate Christ's life *after* he was saved. Look carefully at what Paul wrote in his second letter to Timothy:

All Scripture is inspired by God and is profitable for *teaching*, for rebuking, for *correcting*, for *training* in righteousness (2 Timothy 3:16, emphasis added).

Step One: Learn God's Word

To grow spiritually, there are two foundational steps you must take. First, you must allow God's Word to penetrate your heart. The apostle Peter wrote that as newborn Christians we must desire "spiritual milk" so that we'll grow in our salvation experience (1 Peter 2:2). This "spiritual milk" is the Word of God. As we grow in our Christian experience, we can feed on what Paul called "solid food," meaning the deeper truths in Scripture (1 Corinthians 3:2).

To what extent are you learning God's truths in the Bible not just with your head, but also with your heart?

Here's another powerful verse of Scripture to think about:

For the word of God is living and effective and sharper than any two-edged sword, penetrating as far as to divide soul, spirit, joints, and marrow; it is a judge of the ideas and thoughts of the heart (Hebrews 4:12).

Step Two: Fellowship with Other Christians

The second foundational step is to be in fellowship with other believers in Christ. In the first church in Jerusalem, believers devoted themselves to the Word of God, but they also continued in *fellowship* with others (see Acts 2:42). They were involved in each other's lives. This is why we read in the book of Hebrews:

And let us be concerned about one another in order to promote love and good works, not staying away from our meetings, as some habitually do, but *encouraging each other*, and all the more as you see the day drawing near (Hebrews 10:24-25, emphasis added).

To what extent are you having God-honoring fellowship with other Christians?

PRINCIPLE TO LIVE BY
THE POWER OF GOD'S WORD

To develop a good reputation, you must allow God's Word to penetrate your heart and change your life as you meet with others to study the Word of God and to have Christian fellowship.

GOD'S WORD AND A SHIP

Imagine that you are on an adventure, sailing a ship around the world. There are many dangers involved in a journey like this. You need to be well prepared so the journey will be a success and you will get to your destination safely. But three things in particular have to be working perfectly, or your adventure will end in disaster:

1. First, you must have an excellent navigation system so that you can stay on course.
2. Second, your hull must be sound, without any defects, so that you can weather the forces of nature and the ocean.
3. Third, you must have a faithful crew.

Our Navigation System

God's Word is given to us as the compass on our adventure in this world. The Bible provides direction for our lives and lets us know when we are getting off course. The truths revealed by God and recorded in the Bible teach us how to live life. By following these truths, we are able to avoid the natural disasters that life presents. We are able to navigate through or around these storms, stay the course and safely reach our destination, discerning God's will in our lives and living for Him.

A Strong Hull

Following through on our sailing illustration, the truths in the Bible are "structurally sound," and they are created to give us strength. All of biblical truth works in unison to bind our ship together. Based on all the truths of Scripture, the integrity of our ship's hull is complete and solid. It can withstand the elements that our enemy uses to pound the sides of our ship, trying to crush its hull.

God's Word is complete and whole. It helps us evaluate the variety of messages we hear from the world. When you hear something that is contrary to what the Bible teaches, you are immediately faced with a decision of staying true to God or weakening the hull on your "ship of life" and accepting the bilge of the world's false messages.

For example, one of your friends or an adult may tell you that it is okay to have sex before marriage if you really love the other person. You can evaluate that statement based on Scripture and see that the Bible leaves no room for this statement to be true. The sexual relationship is designed to be expressed between only one man and only one woman, for life. It is meant for marriage and only marriage. It is not to be experienced during engagement or before you say, "I do." (We'll develop this biblical truth more fully in unit 7.)

A Faithful Crew

Ships are not designed to be sailed by only one person. A crew is assembled to work together and support each other in order to reach the ship's destination. Just so, God did not create any one of us to go through life on our own. He tells us throughout the New Testament that we are to meet together, encourage each other, pray for each other, admonish one another and love one another. Most importantly, we are to look to our one and only Captain, Jesus, and follow His teachings.

A PRACTICAL PROJECT

Review the "principle to live by" in this chapter. In order to develop a good reputation, how can you and your Christian friends apply this principle in each of the following areas?

Ideas and suggestions for learning the Word of God:

_____

_____

_____

_____

_____

_____

Ideas and suggestions for having Christian fellowship:

_____

_____

_____

_____

_____

_____

6

Reflecting Christ's Life

PRINCIPLE TO LIVE BY

In order to be an example to others, you must develop
Christlike character traits.

Becoming like Jesus Christ is a lifetime process—especially when a person
has been living out of the will of God most of his life. This was certainly true
of most of the believers in Ephesus. They had been pagan idolaters who
worshiped Diana, a fertility goddess. By God's standards, they were immoral, unethical and living a sinful life in many ways.

Timothy's challenge was to both model with his life and teach these
believers "the truth" that "is in Jesus." They were to change their "former
way of life" and to "put on the new man, the one created according to God's
[likeness] in righteousness and purity of the truth" (Ephesians 4:22,24).

Timothy had probably read this paragraph in the Ephesians letter
many times in the church meetings in Ephesus. However, when he received
his first personal letter from Paul (see 1 Timothy), he understood more
fully what it means to live like Jesus.

What does the life of this kind of Christian look like? The qualities
that Paul listed in his first letter to Timothy answer this question, not only
for spiritual leaders but also for all Christians.

MORAL PURITY (1 TIMOTHY 3:2B)

When Paul used the phrase "the husband of one wife" in this passage, it
may appear that this characteristic did not apply to Timothy, as he was a
single young man. However, a more careful look at what Paul meant applies to men who are married or who are planning to get married or who are
single and even plan to stay single. In essence, Paul was referring to moral
purity. Furthermore, it's not accidental that he included this quality of maturity immediately after stating that a Christian should be "above reproach"—meaning that he has a good reputation. This indicates that one

of the most significant ways we develop this kind of reputation as a Christian man—young or old—is to be sexually pure.

Unfortunately, there are many young men today who have bad reputations because of their relationships with the opposite sex. You've met them, talked with them and even heard them brag about their sexual exploits. This, of course, should never be true of a Christian. Since Paul included "purity" in his list when he challenged Timothy to "be an example" (1 Timothy 4:2), we'll look at this characteristic much more carefully in unit 7 of this study.

To what extent are you becoming more and more like Jesus in your moral attitudes and actions?

SELF-CONTROLLED (1 TIMOTHY 3:2C)

Paul used an illustration in his letter to the Thessalonians to help them—and us—understand what it means to be "self-controlled." We are not to live like people who have had too much to drink. Their speech is slurred and they are physically unsteady. When this happens, they are certainly not living self-controlled, sober or temperate lives.

Paul then applied this illustration. His basic point did not refer to drinking too much alcohol, although he addressed this issue later, and so will we. Rather, Paul was teaching that Christians must be clear-minded and always alert. We must not allow the things of this world to dull our thinking about what is right and wrong. This is a daily challenge for all of us!

To what extent are you becoming more and more like Jesus in your ability to think clearly about God's will for your life?

SENSIBLE (1 TIMOTHY 3:2D)

In order to be a man, young or old, who measures up to the spiritual stature of Christ, we must be "sensible." A phrase that describes this quality is having a sound mind or good judgment. Perhaps the best explanation regarding what Paul had in mind is when he referred to this quality of maturity in his letter to the Romans:

For by the grace given to me, I tell everyone among you *not to think of himself more highly than he should think.* Instead, *think sensibly* [with a sound mind], as God has distributed a measure of faith to each one (Romans 12:3, emphasis added).

To what extent are you becoming more and more like Jesus in overcoming prideful behavior?

RESPECTABLE (1 TIMOTHY 3:2E)

The English word "respectable" is translated from the New Testament word *kosmios,* and is also a word related to our English word "cosmetics." When we compare the pronunciation of these two words—one in Greek, and the other in English—we can easily see the connection: *kosmios* equals *cosmetics.*

This leads to a very intriguing question. How are "cosmetics" related to being *kosmios* or "respectable"? To answer this question, stop and think what cosmetics are designed to do. They make us look good, smell good and be attractive to other people. Consequently, *kosmios* equals *cosmetics* equals *respectable.*

Paul was saying, then, that when we live "respectable" lives before others, the way we live will be like "cosmetics" to the message of the Word of God. Our Christian lifestyle will make God's message attractive to others because we are living lives of integrity and honesty.

To what extent are you becoming more and more like Jesus in making God's message of salvation something others want in their own lives?

NOT ADDICTED TO WINE (1 TIMOTHY 3:3A)

Alcoholism was a serious problem in the Roman world. Not only did men and women engage in flagrant immorality in the pagan temples, but "eating" and "drinking" were also part of their licentious activities. They gorged themselves on the meat they were offering to idols and drank wine until they were often in a drunken stupor.

People who are addicted to alcohol are very vulnerable to making bad judgments in all of their relationships. Men particularly become abusive to their wives and children. This helps explain why Paul followed up this character trait by saying that a man who is mature in Christ is not a bully. Rather, he is to be "gentle" and "not quarrelsome" (1 Timothy 3:3).

Sadly, many young people drink alcoholic beverages regularly and to the point that they lose control of their senses and inhibitions. This often leads to sexual immorality, fights and serious accidents, as illustrated in most teen movies today. In fact, as we were writing this book, we heard of a terrible tragedy. A young man was driving a car under the influence of alcohol, lost control and hit a tree. A teenage girl was killed and her friend was paralyzed from the neck down. A third passenger was left in critical condition. Though the driver was basically unharmed, he was charged with manslaughter. What a tragic event!

Though drinking is a serious problem among young people today, it is only one form of drugs that is used and abused. These drugs lead to compulsions that are even worse than alcoholic addictions. In fact, they often lead to multiple addictions that actually lead to mental and emotional deterioration and death.

---

*To what extent are you becoming more and more like
Jesus in your ability to refuse substances that dull your thinking and cause
you to do things that violate God's will?*

NOT A BULLY (1 TIMOTHY 3:3B)

As we noted earlier, alcohol and other drugs lead to violence against others. This happened in the New Testament world. Consequently, Paul wrote that a mature man of any age will not be a "bully."

Unfortunately, young people in our society today are more and more becoming bullies who gang up on others and become verbally and physically abusive. Many of us have seen these horrible scenes that have even been posted on Facebook and YouTube—such as several teenage girls pushing and kicking another girl. In one case, a young woman committed suicide because of horrible verbal abuse by her peers. Unfortunately, young men are becoming even more violent. Sadly, this type of behavior also results in drive-by shootings and other forms of violence and murder.

---

*To what extent are you becoming more and more like Jesus in
treating others with deep respect and sincerity?*

GENTLE, NOT QUARRELSOME (1 TIMOTHY 3:3C)

Being "gentle" and "not quarrelsome" are the extreme opposite of those characteristics associated with being a "bully." When writing to Titus regarding these characteristics, Paul stated that we are not to be "quick-tempered" (Titus 1:7).

This introduces us to the emotion we call "anger," which is a normal feeling. We all get angry. But when we do, we are not to allow this God-created feeling to cause us to sin against others. This is why Paul wrote the following to the Ephesians:

> *Be angry and do not sin.* Don't let the sun go down on your anger, and don't give the Devil an opportunity (Ephesians 4:26-27, emphasis added).

When does anger become sinful? This certainly happens when we hurt others physically and emotionally, and when we become vengeful and allow these feelings to turn into bitterness. However, this is such an important question that we'll address it later when we discuss being an example with our words.

To what extent are you becoming more and more like Jesus in your ability to control your anger?

NOT GREEDY (1 TIMOTHY 3:3D)

Here Paul used one Greek word that is translated "not greedy." In other words, we should not love money.

Understand that Paul was not saying that to have money is wrong. He clarified this at the end of this letter to Timothy when he wrote: "For the *love of money* is a root of all kinds of evil" (1 Timothy 6:10a, emphasis added).

To what extent are you becoming more and more like Jesus in your ability to be generous with your material blessings?

Unfortunately, people who have lots of money often *love* it. They allow their love of material possessions to come before their love of God. However, this does not have to happen if we learn to be generous and use money to serve God and help others.

PRINCIPLE TO LIVE BY
CHRISTLIKE QUALITIES

In order to be an example to others, you must develop Christlike character traits.

WALKING THE TALK . . . WORK OUT YOUR SALVATION

Wow, this is a challenging list! Don't you wish that Paul had left something off? It takes a lot of effort to do well with some of these qualities, much less all of them, and at the same time.

However, this principle based on Paul's list of qualities gives us the opportunity to look more closely at our character. What is God laying on your heart and showing you? What negative characteristics does He want you to change? What character qualities does He want you to practice more fully?

A PRACTICAL ASSIGNMENT

To help you answer these questions, look carefully at the following list:

- ❑ Moral purity
- ❑ Self-control
- ❑ Sensible
- ❑ Respectable
- ❑ Not addicted
- ❑ Not a bully
- ❑ Gentle, not quarrelsome
- ❑ Not greedy

First, check those qualities you feel good about. Then thank God that He has helped you develop these qualities.

Second, check at least one quality where you would like to improve.

Third, ask God to give you the strength, the conviction and the commitment to make the necessary changes to reflect this one quality in your life.

Fourth, share this goal as a prayer request with a close and trusted friend or mentor, and ask that person to pray for you and help you be accountable.

GOING DEEPER

My dad, Gene Getz, has written a book titled *The Measure of a Man,* which I recommend that you read. The entire book is based on this maturity profile in 1 Timothy 3 and Titus 1. God has used this book greatly in the lives of men throughout the world. In fact, it has been translated into many languages, because it is a *biblical* profile. I personally studied this book with a group of young men. It helped all of us become more like Jesus Christ, and I know it will help you too!

UNIT 3

Watch Your Words

No one should despise your youth; instead, you should be
an example to the believers in speech . . .
1 TIMOTHY 4:12

Words are one of God's greatest gifts to all of us. In fact, this is how He has communicated His will to all human beings. In the 66 books of the Bible, we have the very *words of God*! It shouldn't surprise us that Paul immediately encouraged Timothy to be an example in the way he spoke to others.

What you will read in the next three chapters has been written to help you be an example to others in what you say. You'll also discover three dynamic principles to live by.

7

Communicating God's Way

PRINCIPLE TO LIVE BY

In order to be an example with your speech, you must learn to respond to argumentative people in a mature and godly way, always being teachable yourself.

One Sunday afternoon, I [Gene] received a telephone call. A young man on the other end of the line was angry. He verbally attacked me! Frankly, I had to bite my tongue. I wanted to respond with the same degree of intensity. In situations like this, most of us feel angry and defensive. Has that ever happened to you?

Fortunately, the Holy Spirit enabled me to remember Paul's words to Timothy about being kind and gentle in our communication. With the Lord's help, I told myself to listen and try to understand why this young man was so angry. To be honest, I had to force myself to listen without interrupting. After several minutes, he paused, and I was able to say in a calm voice, "You are obviously very upset."

"I am," he snapped back.

"We need to get together and talk," I suggested.

At that point, he immediately lowered his voice and agreed to meet the next day—which also gave both of us 24 hours to reflect on what had just happened. Time *does* give us perspective.

When we met, he was in an entirely different mood. What he shared was also very different. He told me he had experienced some very difficult challenges over the last several days, leading to his outburst—losing his job, having a serious disagreement with his wife, failing to do well on a test at school and some other traumatic experiences. I sympathized with his problems but reminded him that if he had shared these honest reasons with me when he called, it would have been much easier for both of us.

Rather than talking, this young man began to listen. Eventually, he responded. Through tears, he thanked me for "loving him enough" to confront him with his problem. Those were his words!

At that moment, I understood more clearly Paul's words to Timothy. Because of my gentle, sensitive and yet firm response, I was "able to teach" this young man the truth about his own motives. Had I responded with anger the day before, we probably would have gotten into an argument and I would have missed a wonderful opportunity.

"ABLE TO TEACH"

This quality—"able to teach"—is one of the character qualities Paul listed in the maturity profile in his first letter to Timothy (1 Timothy 3:2g). We've included it here since we normally use words to communicate with each other.

Timothy faced some serious verbal challenges in Ephesus. In some cases, they could have become verbal wars. There were arrogant men who were using words to create "disputes and arguments." As a result, this led to "envy, quarreling, slanders, evil suspicions, and constant disagreement among men whose minds are depraved and deprived of the truth" (1 Timothy 6:4-5).

Non-defensive

In Paul's second letter to Timothy, he explained very specifically how to respond to those who simply want to argue. We should use words in a non-defensive and sensitive way, hoping to be able to teach God's truth to those men—young or old—who oppose God's message. Thus Paul wrote:

> The Lord's slave must not quarrel, but must be gentle to everyone, *able to teach*, and patient, instructing his opponents with gentleness. Perhaps God will grant them repentance to know the truth (2 Timothy 2:24-25, emphasis added).

This is a very powerful passage of Scripture that demonstrates how to be a *good example* in your speech—especially among those who disagree with the message of the Bible. In essence, Paul was saying, "Don't argue, but simply respond in a gentle, patient and sensitive way." This, of course, is easier said than done. But, with God's help, it is possible.

Avoids Arguments

Look again at what Paul wrote and note the various words that describe how to be "able to teach" those who oppose the truth:

> The Lord's slave [servants] must *not quarrel*, but must be *gentle to everyone*, able to teach, and *patient*, instructing his opponents with *gentleness* (2 Timothy 2:24-25a, emphasis added).

When someone disagrees with you in an argumentative way, your natural tendency is to respond in the same way. This, Paul said, will lead to a quarrel. When this happens, communication breaks down. People are not listening to each other. In essence, Paul was telling Timothy that being argumentative is not being a good example in speech.

When is the last time you got into a serious argument, and why did it happen?

Is Perceptive

How can you avoid arguments, particularly when you are talking with someone who is angry? The way you perceive and understand what is happening in these difficult situations is a key to responding with patience. Note the following Proverbs:

A patient person [shows] *great understanding*, but a quick-tempered one promotes foolishness (Proverbs 14:29, emphasis added).

The intelligent person restrains his words, and one who keeps a cool head is *a man of understanding* (Proverbs 17:27, emphasis added).

These proverbs teach us that when people want to argue with us, we should ask God to help us understand *why* they are so intense emotionally. What are their motives? If you can view the situation from the other person's point of view, it will help you to be patient and kind in your responses, even though you may disagree. With the Holy Spirit's help, this is what I was able to do when the young man called me that day and began to rant and rave.

AN ANGRY DRIVER

Here is another powerful proverb: "A gentle answer turns away anger, but a harsh word stirs up wrath" (Proverbs 15:1).

One morning, I experienced what this proverb really means and avoided a serious and potentially dangerous confrontation. I was a guest lecturer at a well-known seminary, and I was driving a car owned by this institution of higher learning. On the side of the car was a logo with the name of the school.

That day, as I was leaving my motel and heading for the campus, I drove across the parking lot. However, I was unaware of where the motel parking lot ended and the main street began. In my ignorance, I drove right out in front of an oncoming automobile.

I still remember the intense and irritated look on the driver's face as he slammed on his brakes, turned the steering wheel sharply and purposely did a 180-degree turn around me. He then got out of his car and was coming at me, obviously very angry.

I knew I was in deep trouble. However, I immediately recognized that I had made a mistake—which showed on my face. I cautiously rolled down the window and quickly apologized, explaining that I was new in the city and didn't realize I had driven into the street. My soft words combined with my sincere but chagrined look disarmed this angry man. Thankfully, he hung his head, apologized for his anger, got back in his car and drove off.

In retrospect, I believe I understand the situation more fully. He had seen the logo on the car, concluded that I was from the seminary and probably had some lingering anger over some other conversation or event. Perhaps he was simply resistant to the message of Christ. I only triggered that lingering anger. However, my gentle and quiet response diffused his hostility, demonstrating that obeying God's Word was the right thing to do. My "gentle answer" had "turned away anger." Had I uttered harsh words, I would have only stirred up his wrath, and who knows what may have happened.

When is the last time you were able to diffuse anger in someone by responding with "a gentle answer"?

PRINCIPLE TO LIVE BY
ABLE TO TEACH

In order to be an example with your speech, you must learn to respond to argumentative people in a mature and godly way, always being teachable yourself.

When I was in high school, I (Kenton) remember asking my dad if he thought Paul had a reason for listing the character qualities in 1 Timothy 4:12 in the order that he did. To be perfectly honest, I don't remember specifically what Dad said. However, I have reflected on this question from time to time and have tried to figure out why the words "speech," "conduct," "love," "faith" and "purity" are in this particular order. Perhaps I'm guilty of over-spiritualizing this word order. However, I'm convinced that God inspired the very words in the Bible and that it's also possible the

Holy Spirit in His mysterious way directed Paul to write down these character qualities in this sequence.

One thing in particular has occurred to me as I have wrestled with applying this verse to my life and the principles that emerge from our study of 1 Timothy 4:12. All human relationships normally and naturally begin with and are sustained by speech. How we treat each other with our words determines the extent and depth of these relationships. In other words, how we control our speech is a direct reflection of the attitude of our hearts and our maturity in Christ. What we think and what we believe in our souls ultimately comes out of our mouths. This is in essence what Jesus meant when He said, "But what comes out of the mouth comes from the heart, and this defiles a man" (Matthew 15:18).

If you know that you are going to have a conversation that will be difficult, how can you approach this conversation in a mature and godly way?

In God's magnificent way, He used Paul to instruct Timothy regarding how to first of all be an example to the believers in *speech*. Pragmatically, this is the only place to start, because God knows that if we are really going to live a life that is attractive to others, our speech and our actions must be consistent. If we claim to be Christians and do not treat people well with our words, we become a stumbling block to others and ourselves.

SOME PRACTICAL QUESTIONS

What about you? Can you think of various conversations that would have turned out differently if you had responded in a more sensitive, gentle and teachable way?

- What about your conversations with your peers?
- What about your conversations with your parents?
- What about a conversation with a close Christian friend?
- What about a conversation with an unsaved friend?

A WORD OF ENCOURAGEMENT

Don't become discouraged if you fail to get a positive response in a difficult conversation. With the Holy Spirit's help, keep trying to develop this spiritual skill. And remember—some people will respond negatively and argumentatively no matter how hard you try. Simply and graciously refuse to argue. However, avoid coming across as "super-spiritual." If you don't understand what "super-spiritual" means, ask a mature Christian you love and trust to explain it.

8

Avoiding Foul Language

PRINCIPLE TO LIVE BY

To be an example with your speech, you must not use foul language.

After my son, Kenton, finished high school, he had a desire to fulfill a dream he had thought about for several years. He wondered how well he could do as a competitive downhill skier. Even as a Texas boy he had distinguished himself as an exceptional recreational skier on the mountains in Colorado. In fact, some of his ski instructors noticed his natural abilities when he was a preteen and encouraged him to continue to develop his skills even more. Watching the winter Olympics only motivated him even more to fulfill his dream.

He got that chance while he was a student at Baylor University. He joined the Summit County Racing Team in Colorado and spent his winter semesters competing. He did remarkably well, negotiating turns in downhill events with speeds that violate most speed limits on super-highways!

Being a part of a racing team also gave him an opportunity to be "in the world" without being a "part of the world." You see, ski racers are normally a breed apart when it comes to worldly activities. I remember one experience he shared with me. He was hard at work doing his training routines—time and again riding the ski lifts in all kinds of weather to the top of the mountain and then barreling down and running the gates on some very challenging slopes. One of the young men riding up with him asked him why he didn't cuss and swear like everyone else. I was proud of his answer. He simply said, "I don't need to use that kind of language."

"Why not?" his fellow racer asked, somewhat surprised. "How do you not do it when everyone else does?"

"I just don't!" he replied.

In essence, Kenton was saying that he didn't have to use foul language to prove to others—and himself—that he needed to be like everyone else to show his self-worth. Perhaps my interpretation is prejudiced, since he's my son; but as I watched him grow up, his identity was not in skiing and cussing, but in being a Christian who could also hold his own on the slopes of Colorado. His primary identity was in his relationship with Jesus Christ. By being an example with his speech, he was getting that message across to his unsaved friends.

YOUR WORLD

Today, you live in a world where foul language is used everywhere—in casual conversations, on the street corners, in local spas and on the school playground. You hear this kind of language in movies, on the radio, on the Internet and virtually everywhere else.

When was the last time you were tempted to use bad language, and why?

Sadly, many children grow up hearing bad language and then imitate what they hear from the adults around them. By the time they reach their teen years, they often have filthy mouths and could care less who is listening. For example, I remember taking my children to a basketball game at a local high school. Sitting a few feet away were several teenage boys spewing out filthy words. They knew we were there and couldn't care less. Frankly, I was very upset. I didn't want my children exposed to this kind of language. I'll never forget Kenton's response—he was just about eight years old then. He quickly reminded me that he heard this kind of language on a regular basis, even in grade school. Sad, but true!

TIMOTHY'S WORLD

Unfortunately, this kind of behavior is not new. The apostle Paul addressed this issue very directly in his letter to the Ephesians—the very people Timothy was to help spiritually. Writing to these believers, Paul wrote:

> *No rotten talk should come from your mouth,* but only what is good for the building up of someone in need, in order to give grace to those who hear. And don't grieve God's Holy Spirit, who sealed you for the day of redemption. All *bitterness, anger* and *wrath, insult* and *slander* must be removed from you, along with all wickedness (Ephesians 4:29-31, emphasis added).

It's not accidental that Paul wrote these words shortly after he addressed the subject of anger (see Ephesians 4:26-27). Though many people use bad words in their casual conversations, their language is often peppered with foul words when they become irritated. It's then that they also take the name of the Lord in vain—a direct violation of the Third Commandment. When God thundered His laws from Mount Sinai, He said:

Do not misuse the name of the LORD your God, because the LORD will punish anyone who misuses His name (Exodus 20:7).

As a young man, Timothy was to "be an example to the believers in speech." Though people all around him engaged in filthy talk, he was never to be guilty of this sin.

A COVER-UP FOR INSECURITY

One Sunday morning as I was on my way to church, I (Gene) stopped by a little donut shop. While enjoying a freshly baked cinnamon roll, I was suddenly jolted by a barrage of foul language. I looked up and saw a police officer standing with his back to me, talking with some of his friends. To my amazement, this officer's language was atrocious. Though he had just gotten off duty, he was still wearing his uniform.

After he left and drove away, I began to reflect on what had happened and why. Here was an officer of the law. He wore a uniform and badge, distinguishing himself as a special citizen authorized to deal with people who violate the laws of our society. Attached to his belt were a gun and a club, giving him authority to enforce the law. And yet, in spite of all these external symbols of prestige and power, he stood there swearing up a storm.

What is this officer trying to prove? I asked myself. *How sad,* I reflected, *that even adult men use foul language to try to build themselves up and make an impression on someone else.*

This story illustrates why some young people also use bad language. Often, like adults sometimes do, they are trying to "prove themselves" to their friends. They don't realize that much of what they say is simply a cover-up for their feelings of insecurity and inferiority. They want so much to be accepted by "the group" that they resort to gutter language to try to achieve that goal. Young men in particular try to appear tough and macho to impress their peers. Unfortunately, more and more women are trying to get attention in the same way.

I'm sure you've seen some of your Christian friends fall into this trap. Some are so fearful of being rejected that they bend over backward to be like their worldly friends in order to be socially accepted. Unfortunately, they sometimes compromise their own inner convictions and "talk" like their non-Christian friends. They don't realize that this eventually leads to a loss of respect—including self-respect—rather than what they hoped for. And it certainly offends our blessed Savior, who gave His life to pay for our sins, especially when you use His holy name in vain.

SEEKING ATTENTION

Some young people use foul language simply to gain attention. This reason is closely related to having feelings of insecurity and inferiority. However, it's different in that people who want attention are not only feeling insecure but are often prideful and arrogant. They want people to notice them. They want to be the center of attention, and what better way—in their way of thinking—than to use shocking words. Ironically, this gives them a sense of power and control; but in reality, they often lose the respect of others, even among their peers.

If you are tempted to use foul language,
why would you say this happens?

> ## PRINCIPLE TO LIVE BY
> ## CLEAN LANGUAGE
> ---
> **To be an example with your speech, you must not use foul language.**

When I was 14 and 15, I (Kenton) had the opportunity to spend two summers on overseas missions trips. I lived for a summer in Sweden and the next summer in Switzerland. I know! I know! Rough missions trips and rough summers!

Seriously, much of the first summer, I slept in an old borrowed tent; and the next summer, we had our own beds in dorm rooms. On both trips we did construction projects for local ministries.

By the way, let me encourage you to consider going on a missions trip. God uses these experiences to serve people and, at the same time, He will work in your heart and life. Talk with the leaders in your church about this opportunity. If you're not attending a Bible teaching church, I'd like to encourage you to find one and get connected with other believers. Then go on a missions trip with your new friends. You'll be glad you did! It will impact you in a positive way for the rest of your life. You'll view the needs of people all over the world differently than you ever did before.

MEMORIZING SCRIPTURE

Okay, so back to my point. While on my missions trips, I was required to memorize Scripture. I wish I could tell you that it was a great joy, but being 14 and 15, it felt more like an assignment and something that I had to do. But the Scriptures I memorized on those trips are etched in my heart. I can't tell you how many times God has brought a verse to mind to help me depend on Him and grow in my faith.

At this moment, as I reflect on the principle in this chapter regarding being an example with our speech, a passage of Scripture has come to mind. You see, the Holy Spirit is still using the verses that I memorized on one of my missions trips.

> Therefore, submit to God. But resist the Devil, and he will flee from you. Draw near to God, and He will draw near to you. Cleanse your hands, sinners, and purify your hearts, double-minded people! (James 4:7-8).

When we look at these verses carefully, we get insights regarding our hearts and our actions. James is telling us to "submit" to God. In submitting to God, we put *our* desires, *our* thoughts and *our* actions in a secondary position to *God's* will. When we submit—and it is hard to do—Satan has to flee. The enemy of our souls can't get a foothold and lead us down a path that leads us away from God.

But notice what else happens when we submit to God. Not only does Satan have to flee, but God also draws closer to us. He will not forsake us. He will help us make choices that will glorify Him and bring peace to our lives.

Every day you can make choices that either lead you closer to God or further away. If you put your brain on autopilot, you'll usually end up serving yourself and actually do things you *may not* want to do!

BEGIN THE DAY WITH GOD!

Train yourself to wake up every morning and say a prayer of thanks. As you go through the day, keep your mind and eyes on God. Always remember that you have to make a conscious choice to depend on the Holy Spirit to strengthen and guide you. I know that if I don't take these steps, the demands of my schedule and relationships sidetrack me from maintaining my relationship with the Lord.

So, is foul language an issue for you? Search your heart! What is God saying to you? What words come out of your mouth when you're with your friends at school, in the mall or at work? What would your friends say about your speech if they read this chapter?

Are you willing to look at this area of your life? In chapter 7, you saw how your speech is a reflection of your heart. Now you have the opportunity to begin to practice training your heart and impacting your speech.

A FINAL PROJECT

Let's take a look at Scripture and see what God has to say about our speech. Read James 3:1-12:

- What does this passage say about your tongue?
- How important is it that you control your speech?
- If you don't control your tongue, what is often the outcome?
- Can you think of a time when you started a "fire" with your tongue?
- How could you have handled the situation differently?
- Do you need to go to someone and ask forgiveness because you've hurt him or her with your speech?

A SPECIFIC PRAYER

We'd like to encourage you to memorize David's prayer in Psalm 9:14:

May the words of my mouth and the meditation of my heart be acceptable to You, LORD, my rock and my Redeemer.

We would also like to encourage you to especially pray David's prayer in these situations:

- When you awaken each morning
- Before you enter the locker room
- While you are playing football, basketball, baseball or soccer
- When you are going to be with your friends in a social setting
- When you are tempted to use foul language

If you pray this prayer, you'll discover that God will help you to be an example in speech.

A FINAL QUESTION

At what other times do you need to pray David's prayer?

9

Encouraging One Another

To be an example with your speech, you must look for natural opportunities to use words that will encourage others.

Though I (Gene) was only six years old and in the first grade, I remember an experience as if it happened yesterday. My teacher, Miss Olive Owens, went to the chalkboard and wrote the word "me" in beautiful cursive. All of us understood this word, since we had learned to say "Me! Me!" from the time we began to talk. But most of us had never seen this kind of writing before. I'm sure that sounds strange to you, but we didn't have preschool classes in those days, nor did we have children's programs on television or those wonderful children's books that teach children to read as soon as they learn to talk.

After writing "me" on the chalkboard, Miss Owens asked all of us to take our pencils and copy the word. I vividly remember looking at what she wrote and then trying to transcribe it on my yellow pad. Since I had never written before, I was getting very frustrated. Try as I might, I couldn't get my pencil to cooperate.

Then it happened! My teacher started down the first row of desks, looking at each child's work. The closer she got to me the more anxious I became. I noticed that when she looked at the other children's work, she patted them on the head to let them know she was pleased. But what would she think of me and my pitiful efforts?

I soon found out. She paused at my desk, looking at what I had *tried* to write. It was a scribbled mess! I was scared to death. What would my teacher say?

At that moment, I burst into tears. But I'll never forget Miss Owens's response as long as I live! She sensed immediately that I was frightened, fearful and embarrassed. She leaned over and whispered in my ear, so that no one else could hear, "That's all right, Gene." She then sealed her words with a kiss on my cheek. You can imagine the emotional release I felt. I was able to dry my tears and try again.

Stop and think for a moment what would have happened if she had scolded me—if she had made fun of me. What if she had said for all the other children to hear, "Gene, big boys don't cry"? Needless to say, my embarrassment would have multiplied—something that I already felt.

To demonstrate the impact those kind and encouraging words meant to me as a six-year-old, here is the end of the story. Years later, when I was in college, my mother wrote to let me know that Miss Owens had passed away. She had died of cancer. At that moment, something happened to me that demonstrates the impact the mind can have over the body. Though momentary, my sorrow for her was so intense that I felt physical pain in my chest. My emotions connected with that unique moment the day she leaned over and quietly said, "That's all right, Gene," and then kissed me on the cheek.

How powerful words can be—for good or bad! When Paul wrote to the Thessalonians, he exhorted them to "encourage one another with . . . words" (1 Thessalonians 4:18). The "words" he was referring to were the very ones he had just written regarding our hope in Christ, whether we live or die. However, his exhortation certainly applies to our words in general and the way we use them. There are several powerful proverbs that demonstrate that we can use words to encourage one another. Let's look at three.

THE POWER OF GOOD WORDS

First proverb: "Anxiety in a man's heart weighs it down, but *a good word* cheers it up" (Proverbs 12:25, emphasis added).

All of us have experienced the kind of anxiety spoken about in this proverb. It's that heavy feeling that comes over us when we are deeply troubled about something. For example, we're disappointed in ourselves because we feel we didn't do our best in some athletic event—a basketball or baseball game, or some other sport. We feel like we let the team down. Has that ever happened to you?

Surviving a Crushing Experience

I remember attending a high school football game. The Christian school where some of my grandchildren attend had earned their way to the state finals. We were in the closing seconds of the game. We had just scored a touchdown and were within one point of tying up the game—which would have sent us into overtime. Our backup quarterback was in position to hold the football for our kicker—who seldom ever missed. All of us in the stands were holding our breath. It was a well-placed snap—but the holder fumbled the ball! We lost the game by one point!

I'll never forget the scene. The young man who fumbled fell flat on his face and lay on the field for a full five minutes while the opposing crowd erupted with joy. One of our coaches finally helped him off the field. What a sad ending to an opportunity to win a state championship, and how unfortunate that one player felt responsible for the defeat.

There is, however, an encouraging ending. The quarterback for the Dallas Cowboys found out what had happened and personally called this young man to encourage him. What a difference this made in his life! Word has it that the whole campus population knew about this encouraging telephone call. You can guess who passed on this information to his fellow classmates. Yes, it's true! "Anxiety in a man's heart weighs it down, but a good word cheers it up" (Proverbs 12:25).

Other Reasons for Anxiety

There are lots of other reasons that cause feelings of anxiety. We hurt someone's feelings and they're rejecting and ignoring us. We did badly on a test in school. We trusted someone who let us down. Or it may be a very serious situation—a family illness or even the death of a close friend or loved one.

Yes, there are many reasons for a heavy heart. I (Gene) remember one experience where I felt terribly confused. I could literally feel the weight in my chest. Obviously, my physical heart had not increased in size. But my feelings of grief and anxiety were so real that I felt heaviness in this area of my body.

Can you remember a time when someone helped you overcome anxiety by sharing some "good words"?

This is why the biblical writers frequently use the heart as a focal point for emotions—whether those emotions are positive or negative. In one psalm, David wrote, "But I have trusted in Your faithful love; *my heart will rejoice* in Your deliverance" (Psalm 13:5, emphasis added). But on another occasion when he was in deep despair, he wrote, "I am faint and severely crushed; I groan because of the *anguish of my heart*" (Psalm 38:8, emphasis added).

Helping a Heavy Heart

In Proverbs 12:25, Solomon was referring to the effects of a heavy heart. But he also shared with us how that anxiety and heaviness can be removed. "A good word" can cheer us up. This demonstrates the power of words.

THE POWER OF PLEASANT WORDS

Second proverb: "Pleasant words are a honeycomb: sweet to the taste and health to the body" (Proverbs 16:24).

As human beings, we are basically two-dimensional creatures—both soul/spirit and body. In the proverb we just looked at, Solomon referred to the "heart," which, in essence, is a synonym for the words "soul" or "spirit." But this proverb also includes the "body." In other words, we are both *psychological* and *physical* beings. Both dimensions are so interrelated that we often talk about experiencing "psychosomatic" reactions.

The Powerful Influence of the Mind

The first part of this word, "psycho," come from the Greek word *psuche*, which can be translated as soul. The second part of the word, "somatic," comes from the Greek word *soma*, meaning body. Therefore, the compound word "psychosomatic" refers to both the soul and the body.

Today, medical science has demonstrated that the mind has a powerful influence over the body. What we think and feel does affect our physical wellbeing. Positive thoughts and feelings can help us feel better physically, and intense negative thoughts and feelings can actually cause our bodies to malfunction. This is what doctors call negative psychosomatic reactions.

By inspiration of the Holy Spirit, Solomon understood this mind-body connection centuries before it was discovered through medical science. This indicates how important Scripture is in understanding human behavior.

A Sick Joke

Three young men decided to give a fellow student—we'll call him John—negative feedback between classes. Just before John entered his first class, one of the three students came up and asked him a question, "What's wrong?"

"What do you mean?" John said. "I'm okay. In fact I feel great!"

"Oh, really! You don't look very well."

After the class was over, the second student met John and called out. "Hey," he said, "you don't look well!"

As John then went off to his second class, he called back over his shoulder, "I actually don't feel good, but I'm going to make it."

When the class was over, he met the third student, who said—you guessed it—"You really don't look well!"

"Yeah," John replied with a dejected countenance, "I don't feel well at all. I think I had better go home and go to bed. I'm really sick."

All this, of course, *was* a sick joke. We should never do it to the worst of friends. However, it does prove that Solomon's proverb is correct: "A joyful heart is good medicine, but a broken spirit dries up the bones" (Proverbs 17:22).

Can you remember a time when someone made you feel good physically by sharing some "pleasant words"?

THE POWER OF APPROPRIATE WORDS

Third proverb: "A word spoken at the right time is like golden apples on a silver tray" (Proverbs 25:11).

This proverb demonstrates how important it is to choose our words carefully and then share them at the right time. Let me illustrate this point. One time, I (Gene) and a friend were riding our motorcycles in the mountains. We were following a winding dirt trail, when suddenly we looked out ahead. There, rising majestically into the sky, were the beautiful twin Spanish Peaks in southern Colorado. We pulled our motorcycles to a stop and took in the beauty.

Can you remember some encouraging words that had an impact on your life in an unusual way because they were spoken at just the right time and in the right way?

We also noticed what made these mountains so captivating. They were naturally framed by a long overhanging branch just above us. To our left was a sloping cliff that formed the frame on that side. Rising up the mountainside on the right were some stately pine trees. To top it off there were beautiful white fluffy clouds hovering above the two snowcapped mountains with the blue sky above them. These beautiful Spanish Peaks looked just like golden apples on a silver tray. I'll never forget that scene. Our heavenly Father had beautifully framed these stately Spanish Peaks. It was an unforgettable scene. Just so, words that are spoken at the right time and in the right way can actually be unforgettable. They too are "like golden apples on a silver tray."

PRINCIPLE TO LIVE BY
ENCOURAGE ONE ANOTHER

To be an example with your speech, you must look for natural opportunities to use words that will encourage others.

YOU MAKE A BIG DIFFERENCE

Growing up as Gene's son, people have asked me the question, "Have you read your dad's books?" I always chuckle and answer, "No, I have *heard* them all!"

At the beginning of this chapter, my dad shared a story with you that I've heard many times. It always touches my heart and brings tears to my eyes. Miss Owens encouraged and loved my father when he desperately needed someone to believe in him. Indeed, they were timely words, "like golden apples on a silver tray."

At the core of our hearts we want someone to believe in us. We need to be encouraged. We need to be loved. God created us to have relationship with each other. Note what the apostle Peter said about our communication with others:

> And who will harm you if you are passionate for what is good? But even if you should suffer for righteousness, you are blessed. *Do not fear what they fear or be disturbed,* but set apart the Messiah as Lord in your hearts, and always be ready to give a defense to anyone who asks you for a reason for the hope that is in you. However, do this with *gentleness* and *respect,* keeping your conscience clear, so that when you are accused, those who denounce your Christian life will be put to shame. For it is better to suffer for doing good, if that should be God's will, than for doing evil (1 Peter 3:13-17, emphasis added).

Peter was obviously writing about how we should interact with people that are opposed to Christianity. But I think that his instructions to treat people "with gentleness and respect" have a significant application to how we are to treat *all people* on a daily basis.

If we are to treat enemies with gentleness and respect, how much more so should we treat our brothers and sisters in Christ with the same degree of sensitivity? If you don't see those opportunities, you're probably focusing too much on yourself and your own needs.

God has placed others in your life for a purpose. They are to encourage you and you are to encourage them. Most often encouragement begins with your words!

PRACTICAL SUGGESTIONS

Look for an opportunity today to use your speech in a way that encourages and strengthens others. Here are some practical ideas:

- Send an email
- Send a text message

- Make a phone call
- Give a hug with a simple statement—"I care about you!"
- Tell someone "Thank you"
- Express a word of encouragement

AN ACTION STEP

After asking the Lord to remind you of someone who needs encouragement, complete the following sentence:

Tomorrow I'm going to contact _____ and share some words of encouragement.

UNIT 4

Live Life in God's Will

No one should despise your youth; instead, you should be an
example to the believers in speech, in conduct . . .
1 TIMOTHY 4:12

Christian "conduct" involves the way we live our lives in all aspects of our
Christian experience. As you read the following chapters and consider Paul's
challenge to Timothy, you'll discover three dynamic principles to live by.

10

Walking Worthy

To be an example in your conduct, you must seek to walk in God's will every day as it is revealed in the Bible.

Think for a moment what you have in your hands when you pick up a Bible. It's an amazing collection of books, reports and letters that were written over a 1,500-year period, by nearly 40 different authors. The Bible is God's eternal Word.

Here's another startling fact you may or may not know. People literally gave their lives so that we could have this wonderful Book in our language. For example, William Tyndale, who lived nearly 500 years ago, was sentenced to death primarily because he translated the Bible into English. Yes, it's the Book you and I read today! Church leaders and even the king of England opposed Tyndale's efforts.

"Why," you ask, "would they do such a thing?" Because the powerful and evil men who opposed getting the Word of God into the hands of the people didn't want them to know what the Bible actually teaches because this knowledge of God's Word would expose their own sinful lives. Unfortunately, this attitude still exists among some religious leaders today.

On one occasion, Mr. Tyndale told a high-ranking church leader that he wanted to make it possible for every young common boy who worked in the fields to know more about God's message in the Bible than many ministers who were trained in religious schools. God helped him achieve this goal when he accomplished the translation of the Scriptures into English; but in the end, Tyndale's enemies sentenced him to death as a heretic.

Think about it! Here was a man who died so that we could have the Bible in our own language. That knowledge motivates me to read and study God's Word so that I can not only live in God's will, but also help others to "walk worthy" of our wonderful calling in Jesus Christ. We hope Tyndale's story touches your life too!

TIMOTHY'S TASK

When Paul wrote his first letter to Timothy and challenged him to "be an example to the believers in speech" and in "conduct" (1 Timothy 4:12), he immediately followed this challenge with the following instructions:

> Until I come, give your attention to *public reading, exhortation*, and *teaching* (1 Timothy 4:13, emphasis added).

What was Timothy to read to this group of believers as they gathered together for worship? What exhortations was he supposed to share? What was he supposed to teach? As you think about these questions, keep in mind that much of the New Testament had not yet been written; and what had been written was contained in a variety of reports and letters in various locations throughout the Roman Empire. However, Timothy *did* have access to one of the most comprehensive and profound letters Paul ever wrote—his letter to the Christians who lived in Ephesus. This letter, and perhaps several copies, was always stored in a safe place in this pagan metropolis.

Again, let's use our imagination. The setting is a large home located on the main street of this gigantic city. As the people gathered, they were following Paul's instructions to speak to "one another in psalms, hymns, and spiritual songs." After a time of "giving thanks . . . to God the Father in the name of our Lord Jesus Christ" (Ephesians 5:19-20), Timothy stood up and carefully unrolled this scroll and began to read slowly and deliberately. When he reached the middle of the letter, he paused—and then read even more carefully and thoughtfully the following words:

> I, therefore, the prisoner in the Lord, urge you to walk *worthy* of *the calling* you have received (Ephesians 4:1).

"EXHORTATION AND TEACHING"

After *reading* these words, Timothy again paused and then began to *exhort* and *teach*, explaining that Paul had devoted the first half of this letter to describing a Christian's calling in Christ (see Ephesians 1-3). He then devoted the second half of the letter to exhorting Christians regarding how to live in view of this great calling (see Ephesians 4-6). If Timothy had access to a PowerPoint presentation like we do, it would look like this:

The Ephesian Letter	
Our Calling in Christ (chapters 1-3)	Walk Worthy of This Calling (chapters 4-6)

As Timothy continued his "teaching," he explained that Paul used the word "walk" to illustrate how we are to live the Christian life. As believers, we are on a journey, and we are on the path that is destined for heaven. At that moment, the Holy Spirit reminded Timothy of what his mother had taught him from the Old Testament. In fact, he had memorized these words from Psalm 119:

How can a young man keep his way pure? (Psalm 119:9).

Later in the same psalm, the author answered this question: "Your word is a lamp for my feet and a light on my path" (Psalm 119:105).

YOUR CALLING IN CHRIST

Timothy may have asked his listeners, "How did we get on this path?" To answer this rhetorical question, he then reviewed what Paul had written earlier in his letter:

For by grace you are saved through faith, and this is not from your-selves; it is God's gift—not from works, so that no one can boast (Ephesians 2:8-9).

If we believe we're on the spiritual path that leads to heaven because of our good works, we're on the *wrong* path. Though Timothy had not heard Jesus teach while the Savior was on earth, he had certainly heard from others that the Lord called this the broad road "that leads to destruction" (Matthew 7:13).

If someone asked you if you are on the right path, how would you answer? (See John 1:12; 3:16; Romans 3:23; 6:23.)

If you could have been there, listening to Timothy teach, he may have turned to you and asked and answered two personal questions: What about you? Are you on the right path? If not, you can be. Think about the wonderful truth Paul explained in this letter. Sincerely acknowledge that you have sinned—like all human beings—and that you need a Savior. Then receive the gift of eternal life by putting your faith in the Lord Jesus Christ, who died for your sins—and mine—and who was resurrected to life by God's power

YOUR GOOD WORKS

Once Timothy reviewed this great truth—that "by grace you are saved, through faith"—he would have quickly reminded his listeners of what Paul immediately wrote in the next sentence:

> For we are His creation—created in Christ Jesus *for good works*, which God prepared ahead of time so that we *should walk in them* (Ephesians 2:10, emphasis added).

> Here Paul used the same basic word he used at the midpoint in this letter when he wrote that we are to "walk worthy." Once we become believers, we are to live in a certain way. We're to imitate Jesus' life in our daily walk. In other words, once we get on the right path—the way that is destined for heaven—we are then to continue on this path and "to walk worthy" of our wonderful "calling" in Christ (Ephesians 4:1). We are to engage in these "good works" that should be developed in every Christian's life.

DAILY CONDUCT

After explaining this great truth about salvation and the good works that should result, Timothy pointed out that Paul became very specific in the second half of the letter in describing how a Christian should walk.

A New Life in Christ

To "walk worthy" of what Christ has done for us in providing personal salvation, we should live in such a way that we bring honor and glory to God. We should respond with deep love and appreciation. Consequently, Paul went on to state:

> You should no longer *walk* as the Gentiles *walk*, in the futility of their thoughts (Ephesians 4:17, emphasis added).

> Timothy would know exactly what Paul had in mind. As a young boy, he had grown up in a pagan Gentile culture. Fortunately, his godly Jewish

mother's lifestyle and teaching provided protection from the horrible depths of the sinful behavior in his hometown of Lystra. She had taught him "the sacred Scriptures" early in life (2 Timothy 3:15). However, he had still observed the way the Gentiles had walked. Even his pagan father had not been a positive example.

Now, as a single young man living and ministering in a "sin city" like Ephesus, even as a Christian he was tempted to participate in some of the pagan activities that were visible on every street corner. Consequently, Paul exhorted him to always be an example with his conduct so that he could freely teach the Ephesian believers how to "walk worthy" of their "calling in Christ"—in this case, never revert to their old lifestyle as unbelieving Gentiles. This is why Paul also instructed Timothy to be this kind of model:

> *Practice* these things; be committed to them, so that *your progress* may be evident to all (1 Timothy 4:15, emphasis added).

What changes have taken place in your life since you have become a Christian? How is your life different today compared with how you used to live?

A Life of Love

Since love is foundational in describing a Christian's conduct, we'll look at this quality of life in a more in-depth way in our next unit of study. However, Paul wanted all of the Ephesian Christians to know that to *walk* worthy of our wonderful calling as Christians, we are to imitate Christ's love for us. Consequently, he wrote:

> Therefore, be imitators of God, as dearly loved children. And walk *in love*, as the Messiah also *loved us* and gave Himself for us, a sacrificial and fragrant offering to God (Ephesians 5:1-2, emphasis added).

In what ways are you loving others as Jesus loved you by dying for your sins on the cross?

To love others as Christ has loved us is one of the most challenging exhortations in the whole New Testament. In fact, it's the basis for being a dedicated Christian. When Paul wrote to the Corinthians, he said:

Now these three remain: faith, hope, and love. *But the greatest of these is love* (1 Corinthians 13:13, emphasis added).

A Life that Reflects Light, Not Darkness

Ephesus was a city of darkness. As we've seen, people worshiped in the temple of Diana, a fertility goddess. Immorality was everywhere. Consequently, Paul wrote:

For you were once darkness, but now [you are] light in the Lord. *Walk as children of light* (Ephesians 5:8, emphasis added).

Timothy was to both model and teach this exhortation. He was never to "participate in the fruitless works of darkness, but instead, expose them" (Ephesians 5:11). What a challenge!

In what ways are you being a light in this world of darkness?

A Life that Is Lived Cautiously and Wisely

Paul's final exhortation in which he used the term "walk" is a warning to be on guard day after day. Thus he wrote:

Pay careful attention, then, to *how you walk*—not as unwise people but as wise—making the most of the time, because the days are evil (Ephesians 5:15-16, emphasis added).

How often do you stop and think about how you are living in this world? What are your personal priorities?

THE SERVICE IS OVER!

Again, imagine this setting in Ephesus. Timothy finished *reading, exhorting* and *teaching*; and once again he rolled up this precious scroll. As the people dispersed, he may have reflected on Paul's exhortations to him in another scroll that was written to him personally—the letter we call 1 Timothy, the one we're studying in this book we've called *The Measure of a Young Man*. Again we can imagine that the following words often gripped his mind and heart:

No one should despise your youth; instead, you should be an example to the believers in *speech*, in *conduct*, in *love*, in *faith*, in *purity*. Until I come, give your attention to *public reading, exhortation*, and *teaching* . . . Practice these things; be committed to them, so that your progress may be evident to all (1 Timothy 4:12-13,15, emphasis added).

PRINCIPLE TO LIVE BY
WALKING WORTHY

To be an example in your conduct, you must seek to walk in God's will every day as it is revealed in the Bible.

GOD'S WORD TO US

Having the whole Bible to read and study is a great privilege. As we've seen in this chapter, when Timothy was ministering in Ephesus, he probably had access to Paul's letter to the Ephesians plus the personal letters to himself. Those letters, of course, represented only a small portion of the New Testament. Timothy certainly never imagined a complete Bible as we have it today. How could he? The invention of the printing press was more than 1,400 years in the future.

We have God's Word today because faithful scribes carefully copied the original Gospels, letters and other books. Though these manuscripts were all written by the end of the first century, the 27 New Testament books were not officially recognized as the inspired Scriptures until A.D. 393. However, Jesus Himself had recognized the Old Testament as the inspired Scriptures, so today we consider both the Old and New Testaments the inspired Word of God. Fortunately, we have this wonderful collection of writings in the volume we call the Bible.

READING GOD'S WORD

I don't know if you have spent much time thinking about the Bible and how God wants you to use it to guide your life. Our guess is that you have been taught the importance of God's Word and that you certainly treat the Bible with respect. You've probably been taught that the Holy Scriptures are not on the same level as any other book, because the words recorded on each page came directly from God. So, why is it so difficult to make time to read the Bible? Why do we not read God's Word daily? In view of the way

God has preserved His message for us, shouldn't we be reading His message and letting it affect how we live?

I (Kenton) let myself get distracted by so many things in my life. It's so easy to crowd out spending time with God. Does that sound familiar? I know there are many things that compete for time in your life too. There are chores to be done; schoolwork to be completed; sports, band or theater practices to attend; TV programs; or, maybe you just think reading the Bible is boring. It just doesn't seem to make sense and you don't know how to apply what you're reading to your life.

I can identify with your experience. A couple of times when I was growing up, I set a goal to read through the entire Bible. I would begin in Genesis and work my way through Exodus, and then I would hit Leviticus. At that point, I encountered some very strange laws, and I quit reading. You see, I didn't have a plan that was just right for me—at my age. So I want to suggest some guidelines that can help you stay the course as you read through God's Word.

PRACTICAL SUGGESTIONS

The following are some ideas to help you read the Bible regularly and apply it to your life:

- **Step 1:** Make a decision to read the Bible on a regular and consistent basis.

- **Step 2:** Find a Bible reading plan that is just right for you. You can do a search on the Internet, using the words "Bible reading plans" and get a full list of resources.

- **Step 3:** Adapt the plan to meet your own needs. For example, if you can commit to three days a week, read those three days.

- **Step 4:** Don't give up. If you miss a day, pick up where you left off the next day. Don't get discouraged; just start again.

- **Step 5:** Choose a version of the Bible that is easy to read. A pastor or mentor can help you make that choice.

- **Step 6:** Journal about what you are learning. You can use the acronym SOAP.

S — *Scripture.* Write down a verse that grabs your attention.

O — *Observation.* Write down what you have observed.

A — *Application.* Write down what you are going to do as a result of your reading.

P — *Prayer.* Write down a prayer to God about what you have learned.

A "PRINCIPLES TO LIVE BY" STUDY BIBLE

At this point, let me make a suggestion that I admit is biased. My dad, Dr. Gene Getz, has prepared a "Principles to Live By" Study Bible based on the *Holman Christian Standard Bible* translation. You'll find 1,500 "Principles to Live By" from Genesis to Revelation. These basic truths are outlined right in the biblical story as it unfolds from book to book. You can choose to read one principle each day or every other day, or even one per week. You'll also find an explanation of each principle and a question that will help you apply this principle in your life.

PRACTICAL SUGGESTIONS

Find an older Christian man who will study the Bible with you one on one (your youth pastor, your father, your coach or another trusted mentor).

Find a friend or group of friends who will commit to reading the Bible with you. Set a time to meet together regularly. Share with each other what you're learning and encourage one another to apply to your own lives what the Bible teaches.

Again, my dad's "Principles to Live By" Study Bible is excellent for this kind of one-on-one or group study! It's scheduled for release in September 2011.

11

Developing Relationships

PRINCIPLE TO LIVE BY

To be an example to other believers with your conduct,
you are to model Christ-centered relationships by practicing
the "one another" concepts in Scripture.

Earlier, Kenton used a ship illustration to help you understand how to live in God's will (see chapter 5). To sail the stormy seas of life, you need a navigation system. The Bible is that navigation system for all of us. You also need a strong hull—God's truth—that will give you the strength and stability to withstand the winds that can drive you off course.

But there is another important element you need as you navigate through life, whether the journey is calm seas or full of churning waves. You need a dedicated crew. You need other committed Christians to keep you from being "tossed by the waves and blown around by every wind of teaching" (Ephesians 4:14).

When Timothy used Paul's letter to the Ephesians and gave his attention to "public reading, exhortation, and teaching," he would have explained the "body" illustration Paul used in this letter to emphasize how important all believers are in helping one another become mature in Christ:

> From Him the *whole body*, fitted and knit together by *every supporting ligament*, promotes the growth of *the body* for building up itself in love by the proper working of *each individual part* (Ephesians 4:16, emphasis added).

SPIRITUAL CONNECTIVITY

In this Scripture, Paul made it clear that each one of us must live in proper relationship with our brothers and sisters in Christ so that all of us can grow together and mature in Christ's love. To show how important these God-centered relationships are, Paul used the "one another" wording nearly 40 times in his New Testament letters. As we look at these exhortations, we can understand more fully what Paul meant when he said that "every supporting ligament" and "each individual part" are important in building up the Body of Christ.

Timothy, of course, did not have access to all of Paul's letters as we do. However, he had heard Paul teach these "one another" truths many times as they traveled from church to church. Furthermore, while in Ephesus, he may have had access to Paul's letter to the Romans. If not, we can be certain he knew the basic content, because he was with Paul in the city of Corinth when Paul wrote this letter. Perhaps he was looking over his mentor's shoulder, watching Paul as he penned each word, especially when he described how Christians are to relate to one another.

While explaining Paul's words regarding the Body of Christ in the Ephesians letter, Timothy may have recommended and reflected on the "one another" statements in Paul's letter to the Romans.

MEMBERS OF ONE ANOTHER

In Romans 12:4-5, Paul wrote, "Now as we have many parts in one body, and all the parts do not have the same function, in the same way we who are many *are one body in Christ* and individually *members of one another*" (emphasis added).

The human body is made up of a variety of members, or body parts—arms, hands, legs, feet, eyes, ears, and so on (see 1 Corinthians 12:14-26). Yet it is "one body." Paul used this analogy and metaphor to show that as Christians, we are a Body that is made up of many members. Just as our human "body parts" are all connected physically, so too are we, as individual Christians, connected spiritually to all other Christians. Consequently, Paul wrote that we are "members of one another." Furthermore, we cannot function properly, and grow and mature in Christ as individuals and as a group of believers, unless we function as "one body in Christ." In other words, we all need one another—young or old.

TIMOTHY'S EXAMPLE

To be an example to all the believers in Ephesus, Timothy was to model this great truth with his *conduct*. Though he was a very important spiritual leader ordained by the apostle Paul through the anointing of the Holy Spirit (see 1 Timothy 4:14; 2 Timothy 1:6), he was also a member of the Body of Christ in Ephesus, and he needed to boldly but humbly function as one of them. Paul explained this "one another" concept when he wrote the following exhortation in his second letter to Timothy:

Do not rebuke an older man, but exhort him as a father, younger men as brothers, older women as mothers, and with all propriety, the younger women as sisters (1 Timothy 5:1-2).

How well are you relating to other members of the Body of Christ—both young and old?

Here Paul used the "family" illustration to demonstrate how he was to carry out this pastoral and teaching role:

- He was to honor older men just as he would honor his own father.
- He was to carry out his pastoral role with his peers as if they were his own blood brothers.
- He was to honor older women just as he would honor his own mother.
- He was to relate to younger women as if they were his own blood sisters.

"SHOW FAMILY AFFECTION TO ONE ANOTHER"

In Paul's next "one another" exhortation in the book of Romans, he actually used the family illustration: "Show family affection to one another with *brotherly love*" (Romans 12:10a, emphasis added). We are not only to function like "members" of a human body, but we are also to function like God designed brothers and sisters to relate to one another in a human family. When we become believers, we are to demonstrate love and affection to one another because we are now brothers and sisters in Christ. We are members of the family of God.

This is one of the most important concepts in the New Testament. You see, the great majority of people who became believers in the Roman world came from terribly dysfunctional families. They had not experienced this kind of affection and love from their parents or among their siblings. However, as they became believers, they were able to join a new *spiritual family* where they could experience for the very first time what it meant to truly respect and care for one another. Furthermore, an environment that was permeated with Christ's love would help everyone—young and old, husbands and wives, parents and children—to experience emotional and spiritual healing. The "family of God" was (and is) to be the "family" that most people never had.

GOD'S GIFT TO ME

I (Gene) was fortunate to grow up in a family in which I felt very secure. Though we were all far from being perfect, it never entered my mind as a young person growing up that my parents might divorce. Though they had their own struggles in their relationship, they were committed to each other for life.

I had three brothers and two sisters, and we all had our family spats. However, we loved each other and would defend each other no matter what. As the oldest, I remember how angry I got if someone picked on my younger brothers. I felt that was my right—not the right of someone else.

You can imagine what happened when we all became Christians! We were more committed to one another than ever. Not only were we blood brothers and sisters in a biological family, but we were also spiritual brothers and sisters in Jesus Christ.

My experience, of course, may not be your experience. You may have grown up in a family where you never heard the words "I love you," nor did you experience it. The good news is that you are now a member of God's family—if you've put your faith in the Lord Jesus Christ. Not only can you experience God's love for you personally, but you can also learn to share it with others. This is why Paul's exhortation to show family affection to one another is so important.

TIMOTHY'S FAMILY BACKGROUND

Timothy probably identified with this "one another" family illustration in a very unique way. Though he had a godly Jewish mother, he had an unsaved Gentile father. As we noted in chapter 3, this may have been at the root of his insecurity and fear. However, Timothy was, first of all, "re-parented" by the apostle Paul who became the spiritual father he never had.

If you have had a secure family background, how can you help other young men experience emotional healing who have not had your family experience?

Second, Timothy experienced emotional and spiritual healing as a member of God's family in the church in Lystra, his home city. His spiritual leaders also became "spiritual fathers." Now, he was a spiritual leader in Ephesus and was to model how brothers and sisters in Christ were to relate to one another. Again, though he was their spiritual leader, he was also their brother in Christ.

HONOR ONE ANOTHER

After exhorting the Roman Christians to "show family affection to one another with brotherly love," Paul elaborated on what this actually meant. They were to "outdo one another in showing honor" (Romans 12:10b). To put it another way, they were to honor one another above themselves.

This is a powerful "one another" exhortation. How could Timothy be a spiritual leader in Ephesus, who was appointing other spiritual leaders, and yet practice this exhortation to honor these leaders above himself? This relates to the concept of servant-leadership, which, as we'll see in our next unit, was beautifully illustrated by the Lord Jesus Christ.

HELI-SKIING IN CANADA

I (Gene) had a unique experience that helped me understand more clearly what it means to honor others above myself. I went heli-skiing with Kenton in the beautiful Kootenay Mountains in Canada. This was a brand-new experience for both of us—but a more intense learning experience for me, since Kenton was a much more accomplished skier. He had already spent a couple of years on a Colorado racing team.

After going through avalanche training—which was a bit spooky—we boarded a helicopter and headed for the top of one of the mountains in this incredible Canadian range. Frankly, my initial experience was very intimidating. I had always felt very comfortable as an advanced skier on hard-packed slopes; but descending through pure powder was a whole new experience for me. The first half-day, I had nearly worn myself out trying to negotiate the very uneven terrain—including a few 75-degree drop-offs.

At noon, one of the helicopter pilots delivered our lunch on the side of one of those incredible mountain slopes. While eating sandwiches and slurping soup, the main guide quietly suggested to me that it might help if I had some one-on-one instruction. He had observed my struggle. Frankly, I was delighted. He then pointed to a rather short man wearing sunglasses, who was carrying empty soup cans to where the helicopter had set down. In fact, he had been constantly serving us food and doing other menial tasks while we were eating.

"That's Waldo!" the guide said. "He'll give you some one-on-one instruction." I was still a little anxious—but pleased. Waldo seemed to be a really friendly guy.

When we took off and ascended farther up the mountain, we reached the top in minutes. We exited the copter, put on our skis and got ready to descend.

Waldo took three of us—all older guys—who were clearly struggling with our skills. Kenton and the other more experienced skiers followed their guide, dropped over the edge and disappeared. I still get "chill bumps" just thinking about it.

Waldo helped me first. Because of my years of experience on hard-packed slopes, I learned some new skills rather quickly—how to bounce through powder and turn on both skis. *Wow!* I thought. *This guy Waldo knows more than just how to serve soup and sandwiches.* He worked with all three of us all afternoon, giving us tips as we ascended and descended those mountains.

A HUGE SURPRISE

That evening, I was eating dinner at the lodge. I was sitting beside one of the older men who had also benefited from Waldo's helpful instructions. He made an unusual comment. "Gene," he said, "my son really enjoyed helping you develop some new skiing techniques today."

My response was a bit startled! "You're Waldo's father?"

After a little more chit-chat, he startled me again. "You don't know what my son does, do you?"

"I guess I don't," I quizzically responded. "I only know that he served us soup and sandwiches, and he really knows how to ski."

Waldo's father then responded rather nonchalantly with a simple but proud grin on his face, "My son is the COO [Chief Operating Officer] of all the Canadian Mountain Holiday operations!"

To let you know what that means, there are a number of these locations throughout Canada that provide incredible heli-skiing. It's a gigantic operation—one of the best in the world.

I was shocked. Here was a man who had been serving us soup and sandwiches. He then spent the whole afternoon teaching us to ski—and not once did he mention his important role in this huge organization.

At that moment, Waldo suddenly appeared with a tray of food and sat down beside us. I immediately told him that I'd had no idea what his position was, and I expressed deep appreciation for what he had taught me—how he had taken time to serve me all afternoon.

Waldo then shared his strategy as a Chief Operating Officer. He would spend a week in each of the heli-ski locations. He would basically go incognito, checking out the services, making sure that everything was functioning properly and that everyone was being served. He also modeled for his staff what it means to serve others, regardless of their positions. He then said something that I'll never forget: "We have a philosophy in our organization. If we serve people, they'll come back!"

A LESSON FROM JESUS

At that moment, I thought about the lesson Jesus taught His disciples that day in the Upper Room when He washed their feet:

> Do you know what I have done for you? You call Me Teacher and Lord. This is well said, for I am. So if I, your Lord and Teacher, have washed your feet, you also ought to wash one another's feet. For I have given you *an example* that you also should do just as I have done for you (John 13:12b-15, emphasis added).

Even though Timothy was a spiritual leader in Ephesus representing the great apostle Paul, he was to exemplify servant leadership. Although he was a primary leader with incredible delegated authority, he was to model to the believers in Ephesus what it meant to be members of one another, show family affection to one another in brotherly love, and outdo one another in showing honor.

How are you showing honor to your brothers in Christ?

**PRINCIPLE TO LIVE BY
SPIRITUAL CONNECTIVITY**

To be an example to other believers with your conduct,
you are to model Christ-centered relationships by practicing the
"one another" concepts in Scripture.

YOU NEED OTHERS

We've looked at only three of the "one anothers" in Paul's letter to the Romans. In fact, Paul outlined an additional five and many more in his other letters. As a pastor's son, I've heard my dad teach most of these powerful "one anothers" on various occasions. Furthermore, I've seen how important they are in helping all Christians live life fully in God's will. I've experienced it in my own life as well.

The importance of living the "one anothers" is true of you as a young man—whatever your age. Of course, I don't know the challenges you face that make it difficult to spend time with your Christian friends. But Paul has certainly made it very clear that you need your Christian brothers and sisters, and they need you. It's only as you minister to one another that you will grow together as believers.

When your best friends are Christians, you share a common bond and belief in Jesus and the Word of God. You can encourage each other to depend on God and look at the Bible for answers when all of you face difficulties in your lives.

It takes time, of course, to get to know your friends. What are they like? What difficulties do they face in school, in their families and in their friendships? How can you encourage them in these areas? What difficulties do you face? How well do people know you? How can they encourage you?

A PRACTICAL PROJECT

We've provided a checklist that includes some of the additional "one anothers" in the New Testament. Check those that you feel you are practicing quite well. Put an *X* where you would like to improve.

- ❑ Loving one another (Romans 13:8)
- ❑ Agreeing with one another (Romans 15:5)
- ❑ Accepting one another (Romans 15:7)
- ❑ Instructing one another (Romans 15:14)
- ❑ Greeting one another (Romans 16:16)
- ❑ Caring for one another (1 Corinthians 12:25)
- ❑ Serving one another (Galatians 5:13)
- ❑ Carrying one another's burdens (Galatians 6:2)
- ❑ Being kind to one another (Ephesians 4:32)
- ❑ Submitting to one another (Ephesians 5:21)
- ❑ Esteeming one another (Philippians 2:3)
- ❑ Encouraging one another (1 Thessalonians 4:18)
- ❑ Confessing sins to one another (James 5:16a)
- ❑ Praying for one another (James 5:16b)

QUESTIONS TO ANSWER

In the area of your relationships, what do you think is the greatest need in *the lives of your Christian friends*?

_____
_____
_____
_____
_____

Regarding relationships, what do you feel is the greatest need in *your* life?

_____
_____
_____
_____
_____

Ask God to help you see what you can do to meet your friend's need(s). Write down what God places on your heart.

_____
_____
_____
_____
_____

Share transparently with God your greatest need and ask Him to help you depend on Him to meet that need. Share this experience with your mentor or other close friend and record any thoughts that result from your conversation.

_____
_____
_____
_____
_____

12

Honoring Your Parents

PRINCIPLE TO LIVE BY

To be an example in your conduct, you should do everything you can to honor your parents without violating the will of God.

At some point in our lives, most of us have had difficulty honoring and showing proper respect to our parents. I (Gene) know I have! Of course, I didn't become a Christian until age 16. But that is no excuse for some of my negative and rebellious attitudes earlier in my life. Frankly, writing this chapter has brought back memories I'm ashamed of.

I *do* know, however, that becoming a Christian changed me! Even though I at times disagreed with my parents, I was learning more about what the Bible says about family relationships, and I wanted to walk in God's will.

TIMOTHY'S PERSONAL EXPERIENCE

While exhorting and teaching the believers in Ephesus, Timothy may have struggled personally with Paul's instructions in the Ephesians letter. Again, imagine listening and watching as he unrolled the scroll and read Paul's words. At that moment, what were his memories?

> Children, obey your parents in the Lord, because this is right. *Honor your father and mother*—which is the first commandment with a promise—*that it may go well with you and that you may have a long life in the land* (Ephesians 6:1-3, emphasis added).

When it came to honoring and respecting his godly Jewish mother, Timothy certainly had little difficulty observing these instructions. Obviously, there would have been times when he thought she was too strict and too demanding in wanting him to follow the Ten Commandments. But down deep he certainly knew she had his best interests at heart when she taught him the sacred Scriptures from childhood. And, of course, she proved to be right. When Timothy heard the gospel from Paul, he became a believer in Jesus as his Messiah and Savior (see 2 Timothy 3:15).

But what about his father? How could Timothy honor his dad when he was an unbeliever and probably a very bad example? Though we're given little information about this father-son relationship, we can speculate from all we're told about Timothy and his family that life at times was not easy, either for his mother or for him.

UNANSWERED QUESTIONS

Did Timothy's father eventually forsake the family and divorce his mother? Did his father die? Did he continue the marriage relationship and at the same time live like other pagan men who had sexual relationships with prostitutes and slave girls? Or was he a relatively "good Gentile man" who honored Timothy's mother and provided for her but simply rejected her faith in Jesus Christ?

What are some of the memories you have in your relationship with your parents that you wish you could forget?

Regardless of the answers to these questions, when Timothy became a believer, Paul would have instructed this young man to honor *both* his father and mother—just as he later wrote to the "children" in Ephesus and instructed them to do the same (see Ephesians 6:1-3).

HOW OLD WERE THESE "CHILDREN"?

In the Ephesians letter, Paul used a term translated "children" that is used in Scripture to refer to offspring in general—whether they were very young or even adult children. However, here Paul was definitely addressing older "children" who were old enough to listen, understand and respond to some very profound instructions. Consequently, when he wrote, "children, obey your parents," he was writing to young men and women who may have been teenagers or even in their twenties and thirties. Many may have been married with children of their own but living alongside their parents in the same family compound, perhaps under the same roof. This was common in this culture.

WHY OBEY?

Paul outlined three important reasons why children should obey their parents. As you read, think about how these verses apply to you.

Obeying Your Parents Impacts Your Relationship to Christ

When Paul instructed these children to obey, he was appealing to the fact that they were now Christians. They were to "obey" their "parents in the Lord" (see Ephesians 6:1). This would have been Paul's counsel to young Timothy when he became a believer. Because he was now a follower of Jesus Christ, he should obey both his father and his mother, even though his father was an unbeliever. Timothy was now "in the Lord."

Becoming a disciple of Jesus should impact all relationships, but especially our relationship with our parents. This raises a very practical question. What if your parents demand that you do certain things that are definitely out of God's will? For example, what if Timothy's father had instructed him to go down to the pagan temple and have a sexual relationship with a prostitute? At this point, Timothy would have a serious conflict between his heavenly Father's will and his earthly father's will. Without question, God's will must always come first. More about that later!

How has your relationship with God the Father affected your relationship with both of your parents?

Obeying Your Parents Is God's Command

The second reason Paul gave for obeying parents is that it is the *right* thing to do (see Ephesians 6:1b). It was God who said, "Honor your father and mother" (Ephesians 6:2a).

As a young man, Jesus set a great example of this; even though He was the Son of God, He obeyed this commandment in an unusual way. When He was 12 years old, His family had traveled to Jerusalem to take part in the Passover Feast. When the event was over, Joseph and Mary were travelling back to Nazareth with their friends and relatives and had been on their way for one whole day before they noticed that Jesus was not in the crowd. They returned to Jerusalem immediately, but it was three days before they found their son. Jesus was in the temple, talking with the teachers of the Law. In fact, His questions and answers were so profound that He astonished these men who were themselves experts in understanding and interpreting the Law of Moses.

By this time, Jesus' parents were beside themselves. His mother was especially upset, and she said, "Son, why have You treated us like this? Your father and I have been anxiously searching for You" (Luke 2:48). Jesus responded with respect, but asked, "Didn't you know that I had to be in my Father's house?" (v. 49).

Luke has recorded that His parents didn't understand what had happened. However, he also recorded that Jesus obeyed immediately and returned to Nazareth with His parents and continued to be "obedient to them" (Luke 2:51). Obedience to parents, then, is the right thing to do. Paul's reasoning was based both on God's commandment as well as the example of Jesus Christ Himself.

---

*Why is it difficult at times for you to do what is right
in your relationship with your parents?*

Obeying Your Parents Brings Personal Benefits

Paul reminded these believing children in Ephesus that when God gave the Ten Commandments from Mount Sinai, this was "the first commandment with a promise" (Ephesians 6:2b). Paul then quoted that promise:

That it may go well with you and that you may have a long life in the land (Ephesians 6:3).

What did Paul mean? To answer this question, we must understand that this was a promise that was given, first and foremost, to the children of Israel. If they obeyed their parents' instructions regarding God's will, they would indeed "have a long life in the land" of Canaan. If they did not follow God's instructions, they would suffer the consequences.

From the total Old Testament story, we know that when parents in Israel faithfully taught their children God's laws, and the children obeyed these laws, they did live long in the land. When they disobeyed, they were often taken into captivity and many were killed; and those who lived were eventually scattered to the ends of the earth.

No, God has not promised that all Christian children are *guaranteed* a long life on this earth if they obey their parents. Some of the most godly and obedient children we've known over the years have died of incurable diseases. They've also been victims of horrible accidents beyond their control. Some have been killed through natural disasters—earthquakes, tsunamis and tornadoes. However, there is indeed a *practical* side to obeying parents.

Though God has not guaranteed a long life, it's quite obvious that disobedient children can often shorten their lives through foolish and irresponsible actions.

Today, we have statistics of the growing number of young people who are killed in car accidents because they were driving under the influence of alcohol. There are those who die because they have abused drugs. In fact, there are young people in prison today who did not actually pull the trigger and kill someone, but because they were there when it happened, they were classified as an accomplice.

There are, then, some very practical reasons for obedience to parents. In fact, when children are respectful and obedient, most parents are more than willing to trust them and give them much more freedom than those children who are resentful, argumentative, and disrespectful and rebellious. This has always been true—in the days of Moses, in the days of Paul, and now in our current world.

What are some of the practical benefits you are experiencing because you are honoring your parents?

PRINCIPLE TO LIVE BY
HONORING YOUR PARENTS

To be an example in your conduct, you should do everything you can to honor your parents without violating the will of God.

SOMETHING I CAN'T TAKE BACK

I (Kenton) remember a conversation with my dad. I was 16 or 17 years old, and I believe it was my junior year in high school. My dad was trying to have a conversation with me to find out what was going on in my life. Through a series of questions and short interactions, I turned to him and said something like, "Dad, it is too late. I really don't need you in my life. You haven't been there while I was growing up, and I don't need you now, except for food and shelter."

Dad is a pastor, and there have always been people who have needed his help. I realize now how difficult it has been for him to balance spending time with family and meeting the needs of the people in the church. As a young boy growing up, I experienced hurt and disappointment because of Dad's schedule. However, he didn't deserve the verbal assault he received from me that day.

When Dad asked how things were going, I had an opportunity to share with him the hurt that I felt. The issue was a real issue, but I didn't share my feelings respectfully. Rather, I let him have it. I was irritated, and I blamed him rather than sharing my pain and disappointments in a sensitive way. In retrospect, I did not honor my dad in this conversation. I shut him out. I was arrogant and inconsiderate. However, my dad was gracious and non-defensive.

What type of conversations do you have with your parents?

FAST-FORWARD . . . SAME ISSUE, DIFFERENT CONVERSATION, DIFFERENT OUTCOME

Now fast-forward about 13 years. My wife, my mom, my dad and I were sitting in the living room of my house. We were reflecting on Dad's work schedule and the impact it had on our relationship.

During this conversation, Dad expressed his regret and sorrow regarding some of the decisions he had made on how to spend his time. He added that now he was making different choices and attempting to prioritize our relationship. I responded by saying that I knew he did the best he could and made the best decisions possible at that time. He then said he was trying to "make up" for his past decisions that had hurt our relationship. Frankly, I bristled!

My mom saw my reaction. She asked me what I was thinking and feeling. Rather than responding disrespectfully, I communicated my thoughts and feelings in a respectful manner. Responding to my mom's question, I shared that I simply wanted to enjoy spending time with Dad in the present because he wanted to spend time with me, not because he was trying to "make up" for the past.

My dad was listening and heard my heart. He validated my perspective and stated that he understood how I could feel that way. He told me that he looks forward to our times together and our conversations, just because we're father and son.

This conversation was a hard, honest and frank one. But it was so different from our conversation 13 years earlier. We spoke graciously to each other and we listened to each other's response.

Don't misunderstand! Dad *does* feel some pain over the past and wishes he could go back and undo some decisions, just like I wish I could undo my arrogant and selfish comments as a teenager. But more importantly, we are honoring each other by listening and acknowledging the heart of each other in our present relationship.

How can you improve your communication with your parents?

GIVE IT A TRY

How well do you listen to your parents? How well and/or quickly do you obey their requests? What is your attitude in conversations? Do you roll your eyes? Do you react defensively?

One way to start honoring your parents is to share with them that you appreciate them. You can do that by saying, "thank you." It might go something like this:

Dad, I have been thinking about how hard you work to provide for our family. I imagine there are days when you would rather sleep in or do something else, but you don't. Thank you. I love you.

Mom, thank you for fixing dinner. I appreciate that you do this every day. I imagine you would rather rest at the end of a long day, but you don't. You work to make sure I am taken care of. I appreciate it, and I love you.

Some of you are probably saying, "You don't know my parents. There is no way I could say that." Well, okay. Start somewhere. Remember, God instructs you to obey your parents and honor them. He will give you strength to love your parents. As you do, their hearts may change! Ask God to help, and give it a try!

How can you express appreciation to your parents?
How can you obey them better and with the right attitude?

A POSTSCRIPT FROM DAD

I remember those conversations well. Yes, they were painful, but necessary. As is true with so many parents, if I had our childrearing years to do over,

I would do things differently. As a pastor, there were times when I was so concerned about other people's needs that I neglected those closest to me. I made wrong decisions. Even people in deep need would have understood my family priorities—if I had explained it and asked if I could postpone responding immediately.

Don't misunderstand! There are times when we must act immediately as pastors—for example, when there's a tragic accident or even an unexpected and sudden death. Our children understand crises if we've established correct family relationships all along. Frankly, as I reflect back, there were many times when I didn't establish proper priorities.

When Kenton stated that he didn't want me to try to "make up" for past failures but to simply "be there for him in the present," a light went on in my soul. I remember thinking, *Why didn't I think of that?*

True, there is a fine line between the two thoughts, but there is a big difference in motive. The first thought focused on *my failure!* The second thought focused on *my son!* It makes all the difference in the world. Thanks, Kenton, for sharing your heart and being honest.

UNIT 5

Love as Christ Loved

No one should despise your youth; instead you should be an
example to the believers in speech, in conduct, in love...
1 TIMOTHY 4:12

This is the most awesome challenge Timothy faced as a young man. The Bible teaches that God is love, and Jesus Christ revealed and modeled that love when He came into this world and died for our sins on the cross (see 1 John 4:18; John 3:16). Furthermore, the Bible also teaches that we are to love one another as Christ loved us! Wow! How is this possible? The following chapters will take you a few steps closer to both understanding and practicing the greatest of all commandments! You'll also discover three dynamic principles to live by.

13

Experiencing God's Love

PRINCIPLE TO LIVE BY

To model love to others, you must understand and experience God's love and draw on His supernatural power through the indwelling Holy Spirit.

One of the greatest challenges I (Gene) have ever faced in demonstrating Christ's love happened when an arsonist set fire to our church offices. It destroyed 15 pastors' personal libraries, including my own. In fact, nothing was left in my office except a pile of ashes. I lost at least 40 Bibles I had used and taught from for many years, including the first Bible I had purchased when I became a Christian at age 16. I had also penned some very significant words on the opening page: "Only one life, will soon be past; only what's done for Christ will last!" Watching everything in my office go up in smoke certainly made this message come alive in my personal experience.

As the senior pastor, I had the responsibility to lead a very agitated congregation to face this tragedy and then forgive the man who did this horrible deed. Sadly, the arsonist was angry because of his own moral issues that conflicted with biblical teaching and truth. How could I lead these believers to forgive this man if I hadn't taken this step myself? As I prepared to face the congregation, I thought of Jesus' words that He shared in the Sermon on the Mount:

> You have heard that it was said, *Love your neighbor* and *hate your enemy*. But I tell you, *love your enemies* and *pray for those who persecute you*.... For if you *forgive people their wrongdoing*, your heavenly Father will *forgive you as well* (Matthew 5:43-44; 6:14, emphasis added).

Though I was angry at this man and what he had done—and rightly so—I tried to view him through Jesus' eyes. I knew I had to love and forgive him before I could lead others to do the same. It was during that very difficult trial that God supernaturally helped me to love my enemy—a man who was full of hate and confusion, and who was desperately in need of experiencing God's love.

Don't misunderstand. I also asked the congregation to pray for justice. This was a criminal act, and this arsonist needed to face those who were charged with enforcing the law. However, this did not mean that we could not forgive him and pray for his repentance and salvation. And as we did, we also reminded ourselves of Paul's instructions:

> Friends, do not avenge yourselves; instead, leave room for His wrath. For it is written: *Vengeance belongs to Me; I will repay*, says the Lord. . . . Do not be conquered by evil, but conquer evil with good (Romans 12:19,21, emphasis added).

THE HIGHEST GOAL

"Now the goal of our instruction is love from a pure heart, a good conscience, and a sincere faith" (1 Timothy 1:5).

These are Paul's words in the opening paragraph of his first letter to Timothy. He reminded his young companion to have one major goal—to encourage all believers to live a life of love toward God and one another and even our enemies. In order to demonstrate this kind of love, Paul outlined three things that create this kind of heartfelt motivation.

1. First, we must have a "pure heart" (1 Timothy 1:5b). A "pure heart" reflects Christ's love in every aspect of our relationships with one another. Paul called this the fruit of the Holy Spirit, which he described in his letter to the Galatians: "But the fruit of the Spirit is love, joy, peace, patience, kindness, goodness, faith, gentleness, self-control. Against such things there is no law" (Galatians 5:22-23).

2. Second, Christlike love comes from a "good conscience" (1 Timothy 1:5c). If we claim to be followers of Jesus and yet violate God's will, we will experience various negative emotions—guilt, remorse and shame. When this happens, it's very difficult to love others as Christ loved us. In fact, if we don't have these negative emotions when we violate God's will, we may have what Paul later described as "consciences" that "are seared" (see 1 Timothy 4:2). We no longer are responding to the conviction of the Holy Spirit. Our hearts have become hard!

3. Third, Christlike love comes from a "sincere faith" (1 Timothy 1:5b). Timothy was dealing with men in Ephesus who were *not* sincere in their faith. They were teaching "empty speculations rather than God's plan" that produces Christlike love (1 Timothy 1:4).

Can you identify at all with Timothy's challenge? How would you feel? It's no wonder that he was intimidated. Who wouldn't be? He was younger than most of those he was to confront. Yet he was to do so by "being an example . . . in love" (1 Timothy 4:12).

Have you ever met someone who talks about love but doesn't live it? If so, how did it make you feel?

SUPERNATURAL STRENGTH

Timothy definitely needed supernatural strength to teach about love, but especially to be an example in love. Imagine how encouraged he must have felt when he read Paul's prayer for the Ephesian Christians and personalized it in his own life:

> For this reason I bow my knees before the Father from whom every family in heaven and on earth is named. [I pray] that He may grant you, according to the riches of His glory, to be *strengthened with power* through His Spirit in the inner man, and that the Messiah may dwell in your hearts through faith. [I pray that] you, being rooted and firmly *established in love*, may be able to comprehend with all the saints what is the breadth and width, height and depth, and *to know the Messiah's love that surpasses knowledge*, so you may be filled with all the *fullness of God* (Ephesians 3:14-19, emphasis added).

God's Love

Paul's prayer certainly applies to all believers. Timothy himself would have been greatly encouraged as he read these divine words that flowed from Paul's pen through the inspiration of the Holy Spirit. His faithful father in the faith was praying for him so that he might experience God's love.

God's Fullness

Note another wonderful truth in Paul's prayer. The only way we can love others as Christ loved us is to more and more understand and experience how great Christ's love is for us. Being filled with the "fullness of God" means being filled with God's love for us so that we can help others experience and reflect this divine love in their own lives.

God's Power

Paul also made it clear that we cannot love as Christ loved in our own strength; however, with God's help, we can allow Him to love others through us. We can "be strengthened with power through His Spirit in the inner man."

PRINCIPLE TO LIVE BY
A SUPERNATURAL EXPERIENCE

To model love to others, you must understand and experience God's love and draw on His supernatural power through the indwelling Holy Spirit.

EXPERIENCING GOD . . . TIMOTHY'S FAITHFULNESS

Dad has already explained that Timothy faced a huge challenge in Ephesus. He was young. He was single. He was easily intimidated. He was alone because Paul had gone on to another place. Yet Timothy was given what seemed to be an impossible task—to lead the Ephesian church. He was to instruct older men and women and help them change the way they were living. He was to help them shape their attitudes and beliefs so they would love each other and pursue God.

What do you think gave Timothy the strength to lead? Why did he stay in the game when He faced resistance and selfishness from the Ephesian believers—particularly among those who were not mature, yet they wanted to be in leadership?

We can only speculate about how Timothy connected with God for the strength to stay the course. Maybe it was his time in prayer, like Daniel (see Daniel 6:10). Maybe it was meditating on Paul's letters. Maybe it was spending time with his closest friends in Ephesus who encouraged him to stay strong. Probably he experienced a combination of these elements. However, one thing is certain! He stayed the course even in the face of adversity. We know that the Holy Spirit strengthened Timothy and gave him special power to remain faithful.

EXPERIENCING GOD ... HOW ABOUT YOU?

Where do you go to connect with God and experience His love? Do you connect with Him through time in His Word? Through time with Christian friends? Through time at church, hearing the Scripture preached and shared? Is it during worship? Is it when you serve others, such as on missions trips or during outreach activities? Or is it a place and an environment?

All of these experiences can help us come to know God's love and sense His power. For me, one of the greatest moments when I connect with my heavenly Father is in the mountains. My senses come alive. I can breathe in the fresh clean air; experience the solitude of a meadow nestled among the pine trees; marvel in the grandeur of a rocky peak, the beauty of wildflowers in full bloom or the power and strength of a storm. I experience who God is and I am reminded of His love for me. I'm also reminded of Paul's letter to the Romans when he wrote:

> From the creation of the world His invisible attributes, that is,
> His eternal power and divine nature, have been clearly seen, being understood through what He has made (Romans 1:20).

Think about it! In the meadow, God knows the location of every field mouse, snake, bird, doe, blade of grass and trout on that mountainside and in that stream. He has created a slice of heaven on earth and is giving me those moments as a gift and as a testament to who He is. Through His creation, I can experience glimpses of His power, creativity, strength, concern and love.

In those moments, I'm also reminded that our time on earth is short. The mountains and the meadows were created long before I came into existence, and they will be there long after I am gone. God transcends my lifetime. Yet, I know through Scripture that He wants a personal relationship with me and with you.

As I sit here in Dallas, putting these words into my computer, I can look out the window and see a live oak tree giving rest and shelter to several black birds. I don't have the mountains as a backdrop. I have cars rushing up and down the street, carrying people to their destinations so they can accomplish the next task on their list. But I can picture the mountains, and I can read the Scriptures and be reminded of God's love.

Take time today and look around you. Where do you see God showing you His love? He is there, and He is showing you His care and concern. Make sure you slow down long enough to depend on Him and gain your strength through Him.

A PRACTICAL STEP

Take time each day to recognize God's love and fill up your soul so that you can give away what God is freely giving you. Take a few moments right now and write down the name of a friend or acquaintance that God brings to mind. What need can you meet or encouraging word can you speak? In other words, how can you share God's love with this person? Perhaps the Holy Spirit will bring to mind someone you don't even like!

A FINAL CHALLENGE

Memorize the following Scripture. It describes our most important Source of strength for experiencing and sharing God's supernatural love. Paul wrote these words as a culmination to the prayer we've just looked at:

> Now to Him who is able to do above and beyond all that we ask or think—according to the power that works in you—to Him be glory in the church and in Christ Jesus to all generations, forever and ever. Amen (Ephesians 3:20-21).

14

Practicing Christlike Love

To love others as Christ loved you, you must demonstrate the fruit of the Holy Spirit.

A number of years ago, someone gave me (Gene) a little book that greatly impacted my life. It contained a single message delivered by a great Christian minister named Henry Drummond. He lived and served God during the 1800s.

This message focused on Paul's definition of love in his first letter to the Corinthians. It was later published and entitled *The Greatest Thing in the World*. Dr. Drummond called these qualities the "spectrum of love," and the message was based on a single paragraph in this letter to the Corinthians, which we'll look at in a moment.

APHRODITE, THE "GODDESS OF LOVE"!

Timothy was with Paul in Corinth when this church was founded. He knew these people well, including all of their spiritual and moral problems. Before they became believers, most of them worshiped Aphrodite, called "the goddess of love." Consequently, the Corinthians were among the most immoral people in the Roman Empire. At one point in time, nearly 1,000 temple prostitutes paraded through the city and made themselves available as part of pagan worship to Aphrodite.

When the Church was founded in Corinth, Timothy saw many of these pagan and immoral people put their faith in Jesus Christ rather than in false gods. He also saw their struggles as they began to understand true love, which in their minds had always been associated with many different kinds of sexual attitudes and activities. Because Timothy was so well known among the Corinthian Christians, Paul sent him—along with the Corinthian letter—to remind them of God's divine definition of love (see 1 Corinthians 4:14-17).

CHRISTLIKE LOVE

The heart of Paul's teachings in this letter to the Corinthians is Christlike love—which he called "the greatest" of all Christian virtues (1 Corinthians 13:13). When Timothy came to Corinth to represent Paul, he would have unrolled this scroll and read a very powerful paragraph that defines love in a very practical way:

> Love is patient; love is kind. Love does not envy; is not boastful; is not conceited; does not act improperly; is not selfish; is not provoked; does not keep a record of wrongs; finds no joy in unrighteousness, but rejoices in the truth (1 Corinthians 13:4-6).

As stated earlier, Dr. Drummond called this kind of love the "greatest thing in the world." When we look at each concept Paul used to describe love, we can understand why!

How patient are you with others?

Love Is Patient

Have you ever prayed, "Lord, give me patience, but give it to me *right now*"? Seriously, it's not easy to be patient, and yet it is one of the greatest reflections of love. Jesus Christ is the greatest example of demonstrating patience, even toward those who put Him to death. When we understand Christlike love, with God's help, we'll strive to be patient—particularly in our relationships with others.

Love Is Kind

Love that reflects "patience" causes us to *wait* before we act. However, "kindness" reflects those things that we do to help others. Again, Jesus is our model. He spent most of His life doing things to help others. He fed the poor, healed the sick and comforted those who were sad. When we reflect that kind of Christlike love, we'll be kind toward others.

How kind are you toward others?

Love Does Not Envy

This was a real problem among the Christians in Corinth. Paul referred to this lack of love earlier in this letter when he wrote that there was "envy and strife" among them (1 Corinthians 3:3). Another word for "envy" is "jealousy."

Most of us live in a very competitive society. In fact, this is the basis of most sports. In the business world, people compete for jobs and position. This is part of life. But how can we love others unselfishly and yet live in this kind of competitive world?

Are you more interested in others than yourself?

With Christ's help, it's possible, even when we are doing our very best and using all of our talents and skills. It's possible even when we are looking out for our own interests. We are to follow Christ's example. Paul expressed it this way when he wrote to the Philippians:

> Do nothing out of rivalry or conceit, but in humility consider others as more important than yourselves. Everyone should look out *not [only] for his own interests,* but also for the *interests of others* (Philippians 2:3-4, emphasis added).

Love Is Not Boastful and Conceited

True humility is also a reflection of Christ's love. Even when He existed "in the form of God, [He] did not consider equality with God as something to be used for His own advantage" (Philippians 2:6). As Paul wrote, "He humbled Himself by becoming obedient to the point of death—even to death on a cross" (v. 8).

Are you following Christ's example in your
day-to-day relationships?

Love Does Not Act Improperly

Here Paul probably had in mind how the Corinthians were behaving at the Lord's Supper. You see, in the Early Church, Communion—as we know it today—was associated with a meal. The "bread" and the "cup" were a part of that meal. Sadly, these Corinthians were still so worldly they were overeating and overdrinking. This was a carryover of how they behaved in the pagan temples. To put it another way, their behavior was shameful and disgraceful.

Love Is Not Selfish

Jesus said that He "did not come to be served, but to serve, and to give His life—a ransom for many" (Matthew 20:28). This is the ultimate example of unselfishness.

What areas in your life tend to bring shame and disgrace on the message of Christ's love?

But don't misunderstand. As Paul reminded us, we all have our "own interests" (Philippians 2:4). However, when we focus on ourselves, we can become obsessed with serving ourselves rather than others. This is why Paul wrote to the Galatians and exhorted them to "serve one another through love" (Galatians 5:13).

Timothy had already learned to demonstrate this quality of love. In fact, when Paul was in prison and wrote to the Philippians, he paid a great tribute to this young man, which demonstrates why he trusted him with these heavy ministry responsibilities:

> Now I hope in the Lord Jesus to send Timothy to you soon so that I also may be encouraged when I hear news about you. For I have no one else like-minded who will *genuinely care about your interests*; all seek *their own interests*, not those of Jesus Christ. But you know his *proven character*, because he has served with me in the gospel ministry like a son with a father (Philippians 2:19-22, emphasis added).

If Paul wrote a letter to others about you, how would he describe your character?

Love Is Not Provoked

Here Paul was talking about anger that is out of control. We've already discussed this emotion in chapter 7. Anger in itself is not sinful. However, it can easily become sinful when we are "quick-tempered" and allow it to turn into bitterness. In fact, Timothy certainly addressed this spiritual issue with the Ephesians when he read from the letter addressed to them:

> *Be angry and do not sin*. Don't let the sun go down on your anger, and don't give the Devil an opportunity (Ephesians 4:26-27, emphasis added).

When we love as Christ loved, we should always keep this God-created emotion under control. And when we violate God's will, we should be quick to ask forgiveness, another great truth that Timothy addressed when he continued to read from the Ephesians letter:

> All bitterness, anger and wrath, insult and slander must be removed from you, along with all wickedness. And be kind and compassionate to one another, forgiving one another, just as God also forgave you in Christ (Ephesians 4:31-32).

Are you allowing your anger to become sinful?

Love Does Not Keep Records of Wrongs

When we are unforgiving, we are not reflecting this quality of love. We are holding a grudge. We've let the "sun go down on" our "anger." This does not mean that we can remove from our memory all the wrong things done to us. Rather, when we become angry, we don't become vindictive and allow any wrongdoing to become the basis of retaliation. We are not to "be conquered by evil," but to "conquer evil with good" (Romans 12: 21).

---

*Are you harboring resentment toward another person and looking
for an opportunity to avenge yourself?*

Love Rejoices in the Truth

The quality of love Paul described with this statement has two dimensions. On the one hand, when we are reflecting Christlike love, we overcome the temptation to be happy when someone is hurting or failing or is a victim of some painful rumor. Rather, we are elated when the truth prevails. As Jesus said, "the truth will set you free" (John 8:32)!

---

*Do you have a sense of satisfaction or joy when someone
is in trouble, or does that make you sad?*

THE FRUIT OF THE HOLY SPIRIT

As you reflect on this definition of love, compare those qualities with what Paul described as the "fruit of the Spirit" in his letter to the Galatians.

"Love" is mentioned first, and some believe the rest of the qualities are an explanation of how love is manifested when we are living by the Spirit:

> But the fruit of the Spirit is love, joy, peace, patience, kindness, goodness, faith, gentleness, self-control. Against such things there is no law (Galatians 5:22-23).

PRINCIPLE TO LIVE BY
CHRISTLIKE LOVE

To love others as Christ loved you, you must demonstrate the fruit of the Holy Spirit.

REMEMBER . . . GOD IS STILL WORKING ON US

As I've read what Dad has written in this chapter, I'm reminded that God is not finished with me yet! There are days when I feel pretty good about the way I've demonstrated these qualities. However, there are days when I find it hard to even look at this list of characteristics, because I know I've blown it. That is why I need to remember and revisit the words Paul wrote to the Philippians:

> I am sure of this, that He who started a good work in you will carry it on to completion until the day of Christ Jesus (Philippians 1:6).

God is continuing to shape our character. I don't know about you, but when I encounter a hurtful person, my first thoughts and responses are usually not God's description of love. That is why we need the Holy Spirit's help to live faithfully. He continues to work in our hearts and lives, even when it seems overwhelming and impossible to respond to people in a loving manner.

ONE STEP AT A TIME!

I am reminded about educator and philosopher Loren Eiseley's story of a boy he encountered on a beach. One day the tide came in and then receded and left starfish littered across the beach as far as the eye could see.

This boy was heartbroken and realized that unless someone did something the starfish would die. He began picking up the starfish one at a time and throwing them back into the ocean. As he was laboring in love, Mr. Eiseley asked this little boy what he was doing.

He replied, "Sir, the tide has come and gone and left these starfish on the beach. Unless they get thrown back into the ocean they are going to die. Will you help?

The man stared at the boy and said, "Son, can't you see all these starfish? There are thousands littered all over the beach for miles. You can't possibly make a difference."

The boy reached down, picked up a starfish and threw it back into the ocean. As he did, he looked at Mr. Eiseley and said, "I made a difference to that one!"

The world wants to tell us that no one can live a life of love as described by the apostle Paul. The task is too big; it is too hard. No one can do that. I will be honest. There are many days that this task does feel too big and too hard. I just don't *want* to do it.

But God does not call us to give up. The truth is that we can't do it on our own. We need God's help. We have to ask ourselves, *Will I be the boy who faithfully worked at an overwhelming task? Or will I be the man who sees the enormity of the task and says it can't be done?* Just remember, if we choose to be like the starfish boy, there is a Man who can help us rather than discourage us. His name is Jesus. He says it's possible, and He has promised to give us the strength. He will deliver more than we could ever ask or imagine when we are faithful to His Word and His calling. Don't give up. Take one step at a time!

A PERSONAL RESPONSE

In order to evaluate the extent that you are practicing Christlike love toward your family, your friends and even your enemies, use the following checklist.

Place a check (√) for the characteristic in which you are making progress. Place an X by the characteristic in which you are having the most difficulty reflecting Christ's love. (Note: Be sure to give yourself credit where you are making progress. Remember that none of us is perfect!)

- ❑ Love is patient
- ❑ Love is kind
- ❑ Love does not envy
- ❑ Love is not boastful and conceited
- ❑ Love does not act improperly
- ❑ Love is not selfish
- ❑ Love is not provoked
- ❑ Love does not keep records of wrongs
- ❑ Love finds no joy in unrighteousness but rejoices in the truth

A FINAL STEP

As you look back over this final list, don't be discouraged. Rather, circle one quality in which you want to improve the most, and share this desire with someone who will pray with and for you—a close friend, a parent, a youth pastor or another trusted adult.

Loving One Another

PRINCIPLE TO LIVE BY

To communicate the Gospel message effectively and powerfully, you must love others as Christ loved you, demonstrating that Jesus Christ came from the Father to enable people to be saved.

Have you ever stopped to wonder what it would be like to watch Jesus work miracles? What if you could have been at the wedding in Cana where He turned gallons of water into wine? Imagine watching Jesus heal a lame man who had never walked; open the eyes of a blind beggar who had never seen the light of day; and raise Lazarus from the dead! And then you saw Him miraculously multiply five little loaves of bread and two small fish that fed thousands. The next day you saw Him walk on the turbulent waves in the Sea of Galilee, and with a simple command, He stilled a raging storm!

Here's a question that should get your attention! What if Jesus told you that you can be part of a miracle so great that it will convince people that He is indeed one with the Father; came from the Father; and that through believing in Him, they could have eternal life? The fact is, you can be part of this miracle! Jesus has prayed for you. He has asked God the Father to enable you to be a unique part of this kind of miracle. Stay tuned and you'll discover how this can actually happen.

TIMOTHY AND THE APOSTLE JOHN

Like you and me, Timothy did not have the privilege of talking with Jesus face to face and watching Him work miracles. However, as time went by, he probably met the apostle John who definitely had these experiences. According to some of the Early Church fathers (those men who lived beyond the time period in the New Testament), John spent his final years in Ephesus, where Timothy was also ministering and where he received Paul's personal letters (1 and 2 Timothy).

We're not sure when this meeting may have taken place, since John lived until he was more than 90 years old. However, imagine the scene. Timothy would certainly have asked question after question:

- What was it like to walk and talk with Jesus?
- How did he feel when Jesus walked on water and stilled the storm?
- When did he first know that Jesus was truly God come in human flesh?
- When did he first understand that Jesus came to die for the sins of the world?
- How did he feel when he and Peter were given the power to heal a lame man in the temple complex after Jesus had returned to heaven?

THE PASSOVER MEAL

If and when this meeting took place, we can be confident that John would have answered all of Timothy's questions. He would also have shared that awesome event when he first began to understand what it really meant to love others as Christ loved all of us. It happened shortly before the Savior was nailed to the cross. The 12 disciples were with the Lord in Jerusalem, when they met in an upper room to celebrate the annual Jewish Passover meal. None of these men understood what was about to happen to Jesus even though He had told them He was about to die. They were all in denial.

Self-serving Attitudes

Even after three years with Jesus, these men still didn't understand why Jesus had come into the world—even after He worked miracle after miracle. In fact, tears may have filled John's eyes as he told Timothy that he and his brother, James, were still vying for power during that final Passover meal. At that moment they still believed that Jesus was going to become king in Israel and would free them from Roman rule. As they envisioned Jesus eventually sitting on His throne in Jerusalem, James—the oldest—wanted to be sitting on Jesus' right hand, and he, John, wanted to be sitting on Jesus' left. In fact, even at that final meeting when Jesus explained that He was going to shed His blood for them, *all* of the apostles began to argue about who would be the greatest among them (see Luke 22:24). What an embarrassing memory!

A Humbling Experience

Earlier, Jesus had charged Peter and John to spend the day preparing for the Passover meal (see Luke 22:7). John may have smiled through his tears as he shared with Timothy that they had arranged for the bowl and the towel but had forgotten to secure a servant to wash their feet. "Would you believe," John confessed, "that Jesus patiently waited until the middle of the meal to give one of us the opportunity to volunteer to be the servant? None of us volunteered, so Jesus performed this humble task."

"But there's more!" John continued, as Timothy listened in amazement! "After that humiliating experience, Jesus asked all of us a very embarrassing question with an even more pointed answer." Here John actually quoted Jesus' words:

> Do you know what I have done for you? You call Me Teacher and Lord. This is well said, for I am. So if I, your Lord and Teacher, have washed your feet, you also ought to wash one another's feet. For I have given you an example that you also should do just as I have done for you (John 13:12b-15).

A New Commandment

John would have certainly told Timothy that during this incredible Upper Room experience he began to learn one of his most valuable lessons: the true meaning and purpose of demonstrating Christlike love. Three times following this humble act of foot-washing, Jesus said, "Love one another" (emphasis added):

> I give you a new commandment: *love one another* (John 13:34a).

> Just as I have loved you, you must also *love one another* (John 13:34b).

> By this all people will know that you are My disciples, if you have *love for one another* (John 13:35).

John and the other disciples understood the "old commandment"—the Law of Moses. But they certainly did not understand this "new commandment." They were self-centered men, thinking only about their own positions and what they—at that time—believed would be Christ's earthly kingdom. But with this act of servanthood—washing their feet—Jesus began to help them understand this new commandment to love one another. And if they loved one another as Christ loved them, they would demonstrate to everyone that they were Christ's disciples—and that they were followers of the one who "loved them to the end" (John 13:1b).

TRANSFORMED MEN

Following Christ's death, resurrection and ascension, all of these men—except Judas, who betrayed Jesus—were eventually transformed. They began to understand more fully *why* Jesus had come into the world. In fact, John's brother, James, died a martyr's death because of his devoted love for Christ and His enemies. John lived on and was eventually banished for a time to the island of Patmos, where he wrote the book of Revelation. When he was released, he evidently spent his final years in Ephesus.

During this period of time in Ephesus, John wrote three little letters that we call 1, 2 and 3 John. In 1 John, this aged apostle spelled out clearly the ultimate meaning of true love—something he certainly did not understand during that incredible Upper Room experience nearly 60 years earlier. He now understood what it really meant to love as Christ loved. Consequently, he wrote the following words:

> This is how we have come to know love: He laid down His life for us. We should also lay down our lives for our brothers (1 John 3:16).

LOVE AND UNITY

Timothy certainly learned another great lesson about love—from both Paul and John. Following the Upper Room experience, Jesus was on His way to the Garden of Gethsemane. That night before He was betrayed by Judas, He prayed for the apostles—and for all of us. His request relates to the results of Christlike love—oneness and unity—which is clear from these words:

> I pray not only for these [the apostles], but also for those who believe in Me through their message [all believers]. May they *all be one*, as You, Father, are in Me and I am in You. May they also be *one in Us, so the world may believe You sent Me* (John 17:20-21, emphasis added).

You see, following Jesus' resurrection, He was going to ascend back to heaven. However, He wanted these men—and all of us—to love one another as He has loved us so that we would reveal who He is and why He came. Jesus was one with the Father, and He wanted us to be one with each other, reflecting to all people that He is the Savior of the world. This means that you can be a part of a community of believers who can miraculously demonstrate to unbelievers what Jesus' miracles were designed to do—to convince people He came from God, was one with God and came to save them if they believed He was the Son of God. Love and unity among believers is the primary miracle that God wants to use today. You *can* be a part of that miracle.

> ## PRINCIPLE TO LIVE BY
> ## LOVING ONE ANOTHER
> ---
> To communicate the Gospel message effectively and powerfully,
> you must love others as Christ loved you, demonstrating that Jesus Christ
> came from the Father to enable people to be saved.

SHARING YOUR FAITH

If you've been in church for very long, I'm sure you've heard a message on witnessing. After all, Jesus said, "Go, therefore, and make disciples of all nations" (Matthew 28:19). This includes those with whom we go to school, play sports with and work with. If you're like us, you've often felt a sense of responsibility—and even guilt. It seems like such an enormous task! It can become a burden rather than a blessing.

We've all felt this way. However, we forget what Jesus taught James and John—and all the disciples at the Passover meal and on the way to the Garden of Gethsemane. God has not called us to carry out this responsibility alone or just with our words. We're to demonstrate who Jesus is by our love for one another and with the oneness this creates. This is the miracle God wants to use to convince people that Jesus Christ is the Savior of the world. And all of us can be a part of that miracle that in turn enables all of us *together* to share the good news regarding salvation.

However, there's often a problem. It's easy for all of us to associate with our small circle of friends. But we can easily exclude others. If we're not careful, we create cliques. When this happens, your youth group lacks love and unity; and when your unsaved friends visit, they sense these divisions and the lack of concern for others.

How can you help all of your friends to be a part of this miracle of love and unity?

The miracle Jesus prayed for—that we might be one as He is one with the Father—does not exist as it should. But when it does exist, we are a part of that miracle. Together with others we are demonstrating God's power and the message of the gospel. Then when we share the gospel message verbally, the Holy Spirit uses both our love and our words to convince people that they, too, need a Savior. And even if someone else shares the message, you are still a part of that miracle in helping someone come to Christ. This is what Jesus prayed for!

SCRIPTURES ON LOVE AND UNITY

The following selected Scriptures are divided into two categories that relate to Jesus' command to *love one another* and His prayer for *oneness and unity*. As you reflect on these verses of Scripture, ask God to help you practice these biblical truths in your relationship with your friends.

The Power of Love

"You shall love your neighbor as yourself" (James 2:8).

"Keep your love for one another at full strength, since love covers a multitude of sins" (1 Peter 4:8).

"If God loved us in this way, we also must love one another" (1 John 4:11).

"With all humility and gentleness, with patience, accepting one another in love" (Ephesians 4:2).

"And I pray this: that your love will keep on growing in knowledge and every kind of discernment" (Philippians 1:9).

The Power of Unity

"Now may the God of endurance and encouragement grant you agreement with one another, according to Christ Jesus, so that you may glorify the God and Father of our Lord Jesus Christ with a united mind and voice" (Romans 15:5-6).

"Now I urge you, brothers, in the name of our Lord Jesus Christ, that you all say the same thing, that there be no divisions among you, and that you be united with the same understanding and the same conviction" (1 Corinthians 1:10).

UNIT 6

Develop Your Faith

No one should despise your youth; instead you should be an example
to the believers in speech, in conduct, in love, in faith . . .
1 TIMOTHY 4:12

The word "faith" is used approximately 250 times in the New Testament, and it is used in three important ways:

1. "Saving faith" refers to how we are saved.
2. "The faith" describes what we believe.
3. "Living faith" describes how we are to live.

You'll see the importance of developing these three kinds of faith in the three chapters to follow, and you'll discover three dynamic principles to live by.

Experiencing Saving Faith

PRINCIPLE TO LIVE BY

To be an example in faith, you must understand and believe that you are saved by grace through faith and not by works.

Most of us have heard of Martin Luther. He was a very important person in launching the Great Reformation of the 1500s. Whether we realize it or not, this is a movement that has impacted most of us in a very dramatic way.

Luther was a very sincere monk and Bible teacher who tried the best he could to be a righteous man before God. He wanted to keep the Ten Commandments perfectly; but like all of us, he couldn't! Consequently, when he failed to keep this perfect standard, he felt terribly guilty and deeply concerned about his eternal relationship with God. In fact, when he read about the righteousness of God (God's perfection), he was terrified. He knew he wasn't measuring up to God's holiness. He knew that even though he believed the Bible and believed in Jesus Christ, he was still a sinner who fell far short of God's perfect demands. How then could he ever be saved?

His terror actually turned into hatred toward God. But then one day, the Holy Spirit opened his heart and he understood that our human failures are why Jesus Christ came into this world. We cannot earn our salvation. We can only be righteous or perfect in God's sight by faith when we receive the free gift of salvation God offers to all who believe in Christ's death and resurrection. Martin Luther understood for the first time the complete message from the book of Romans. Though he had taught this book to others, he now understood this very important verse:

For the wages of sin is death, but the *gift of God* is *eternal life* in Christ Jesus our Lord (Romans 6:23, emphasis added).

Because Martin Luther understood this great truth and believed it, he wrote that he was "born again" and his conscience was at rest. Rather than living day after day with anxiety and anger, he was certain of his salvation.

God then used him to help millions and millions of people understand "saving faith."

TIMOTHY'S PERSPECTIVE

As we noted earlier, Timothy may have had access to a copy of this very letter that Paul wrote to the Romans. However, if he didn't, he certainly knew the contents, since he was in Corinth when Paul penned this letter. Furthermore, Timothy understood clearly what Martin Luther *did not* understand for many years of his life.

To really understand "saving faith," it's important to read what Paul wrote in the early part of this letter to the Romans. After describing the sinful condition of all people—both Jews and Gentiles—Paul wrote that "God's righteousness has been revealed . . . through faith in Jesus Christ, to all who believe" (Romans 3:21-22). Here Paul not only used the word "faith," but also the word "believe," which is also used about 250 times in the New Testament and has the same basic meaning as "faith." In fact, the apostle John used this word nearly 100 times in his Gospel. In most instances he used the word to describe *saving faith*. For example, note that great verse in John 3:

> For God loved the world in this way: He gave His One and Only Son, so that everyone who *believes* [has faith] in Him will not perish but have eternal life (John 3:16, emphasis added).

"Declared Righteous"

In this letter to the Romans, Paul made it very clear that no one has ever been saved apart from faith. He mentioned Abraham, who lived hundreds of years before Jesus Christ was born. Though this Old Testament patriarch did not fully understand God's redemptive plan, he "believed" what God promised when he told him that he and his wife, Sarah, would have a son in their old age. From our vantage point, we know that this meant that through Abraham and his son Isaac, Jesus Christ would eventually be born and be the Savior of the world. Because he "believed" in God's promise, he was saved or "declared righteous" by God Himself. To be "justified" in God's sight is another word we use to describe the salvation experience (see Romans 4:1-3).

To be "declared righteous" or to be "justified" means that God sees us as perfect—not because we are able to live this way in this life—but because Jesus Christ became the *perfect sacrifice*. When we sincerely believe Jesus died for our sins, we are saved or "declared righteous." In God's sight we *are* perfect because Jesus Christ paid for all of our sins—past, present and future. This is what Paul meant when he wrote:

> Therefore, since we have been *declared righteous by faith*, we have *peace with God* through our Lord Jesus Christ (Romans 5:1, emphasis added).

"Peace with God"

To have "peace with God" means that our heavenly Father no longer sees our sins as separating us from His perfect holiness. This happens when we are "declared righteous by faith." This does not mean we will never sin again, but because Jesus Christ, the perfect Son of God, took our place when He died, His blood continues to cleanse us from all our sins—those that are past, those that are in our present life and those that we will commit in the future (see 1 John 1:9).

In fact, because God is omniscient and knows everything, He already sees us as "glorified" (see Romans 8:29-30), which means that in His sight we are already seated "with Him in the heavens, in Christ Jesus" (Ephesians 2:6).

God's Free Gift

To be "declared righteous" means that salvation is a free gift. We cannot earn eternal life by doing good works. When Martin Luther understood this great truth, he was, as he wrote, "born again." We can be sure that Timothy made this wonderful message very clear to the Ephesians when he read from the scroll Paul wrote to them:

> For by *grace* you are saved *through faith*, and this is not from yourselves; *it is God's gift—not from works*, so that no one can boast (Ephesians 2:8-9, emphasis added).

A PERSONAL EXPERIENCE

As a young man growing up in a relatively small religious sect, I (Gene) did not understand this wonderful truth. The leaders of the church taught us that we have "peace with God" when we confess all our sins, try to make things right and then attempt to live a good life, hoping that we might go to heaven when we die. Fortunately, my parents began to understand "saving faith," by listening to good Bible teaching on the radio. Consequently, when I received Christ by faith at age 16, I understood that salvation was a gift from God. However, I was still confused. I believed that I needed to keep myself saved by living a good life.

You can imagine my ups and downs. I felt like I was on a spiritual and emotional roller coaster. When I felt that I was living up to God's standard of righteousness, I *felt* saved. When I failed God, I *felt* lost. This continued to be a very frustrating and depressing life experience until one day, while reading the book of Romans, I received the assurance of my salvation. I began to understand more fully "saving faith." It changed my life—which I'll talk more about in the next chapters.

PRINCIPLE TO LIVE BY
SAVING FAITH

To be an example in faith, you must understand and believe that you are saved by grace through faith and not by works.

THE TRUTH REJECTED BY MANY

When I (Kenton) was in the sixth grade, I attended a weekend seminar with my youth group. Christian apologist and author Josh McDowell was speaking. I don't remember most of what he said (sorry, Josh), but I do remember a powerful illustration that God has used as a marker in my life.

Josh used a series of slides to show that all the major religions of the world are based on a system of beliefs that are related to various personalities. However, if you remove the founders of these religions from these systems of belief, the religions would still stand. For example, Buddhism is not dependent on Buddha. Islam is not dependent on Mohammed. Judaism is not dependent on Moses.

Josh illustrated this point by using buildings to represent these belief systems. He put the name of the founder on each building. Josh then removed the names of these various religions from each building and they did not collapse.

He then illustrated Christianity with another building. Like the other religions, he placed the name of Jesus Christ on the building. He then demonstrated that if you remove the name of Jesus Christ from Christianity, the building will collapse. Jesus Christ is not only the foundation of the building, but He is also the basis of our faith. Only Jesus can save us. When the apostle Thomas asked the way to heaven, Jesus responded to him with these profound words:

Jesus told him, "I am the way, the truth, and the life. No one comes to the Father except through Me" (John 14:6).

I will never forget this illustration. Even as an 11-year-old, it helped me to understand in a new way the importance of the centrality of Christ in Christianity. Josh clearly helped me see that all the other religions of the world are based on the belief that man can fix the problem of sin. The Bible teaches that *only* Jesus can fix this problem since He, as the perfect Son of God, died for us. Paul stated it this way:

He made the One who did not know sin to be sin for us, so that we might become the righteousness of God in Him (2 Corinthians 5:21).

TWO IMPORTANT QUESTIONS

This leads to two important questions to consider: Do you trust that you can solve the problem of sin in your life? Or do you trust and accept that God, in His loving character, solved this problem for you by sending Christ to die for your sins and rise from the dead?

The second question represents the truth. It is that simple . . . yet rejected by many. I'm praying that this illustration will drive a stake in the ground for you, as it did for me, in helping you understand that salvation is only attained by grace through faith in Jesus Christ. Salvation cannot be earned by your own efforts as taught by all other religions.

Have you received God's gift by believing that Jesus Christ died for your sins and rose again to give you eternal life?

A PERSONAL PRAYER

Once again, here is a prayer that will help you make sure that you have saving faith:

Dear Father, even though I can do many good things, I confess that I can never do enough to earn salvation. I now believe that I can have eternal life, beginning right now, by receiving this wonderful gift by faith. I now believe that Your perfect Son, Jesus Christ, died for all of my sins—past, present and future. I also believe that You rose from the grave, and because You live, I can live eternally with You in heaven. However, I want You to know that because You have given me this wonderful gift, my desire is to do all the good I can to express my deep appreciation for Your grace and mercy. Help me to live more and more in Your perfect will. In Jesus' name. Amen.

17

Developing Believing Faith

PRINCIPLE TO LIVE BY

To be an example in faith, you must understand and believe the basic teachings in the New Testament about Jesus Christ.

Has anyone ever asked you the question, "What is your faith?" In many cases, they're asking you what religious group you belong to or associate with. For example, they may be asking you if you are a Baptist or a Methodist or a Presbyterian or a Roman Catholic. They also may be wondering if you are a Mormon, a Jehovah's Witness or even a Hindu, a Buddhist or a Muslim.

When the New Testament was written, these groups did not yet exist. However, there were people who had various belief systems that did not measure up to what the Holy Spirit revealed about Jesus Christ and who He is! Consequently, when Paul challenged Timothy to "be an example . . . in faith" (1 Timothy 4:12), part of that challenge was to demonstrate with his life what he believed about Jesus Christ.

THE COMPLETE STORY

After the Lord Jesus ascended back to heaven, and the Holy Spirit came on the Day of Pentecost (see Acts 2), the apostles began to share the good news about Christ's death and resurrection, beginning in the city of Jerusalem. Not surprisingly, many of the Jewish leaders opposed their preaching. In fact, immediately after Jesus arose from the grave, some of the Roman soldiers reported to the chief priests that they had seen a glorious and shining angel roll back the heavy stone in front of Jesus' tomb. Jesus was not there! The tomb was empty.

This was *not* good news for these religious leaders. In their panic, they developed a deceptive plan. They gave the soldiers a large sum of money and instructed them to lie—to report to everyone that Christ's disciples came during the night and stole His body while they were sound asleep (see Matthew 28:11-13). In fact, this "lie" has been perpetuated for centuries in various ways, even though no one has ever found Jesus' dead and decomposed body. Even those who accept the historical facts that Jesus lived and died, but who deny that He rose from the grave, have no satisfactory answer regarding His corpse. It was never found. Those of us who know and accept the total story about Jesus believe that He is alive and has returned to heaven!

When I saw the stage play *Jesus Christ Superstar,* I noticed that the author included many of the correct facts about Jesus' life and death. However, it was very clear at the end of this high-energy drama that Christ's resurrection was omitted. Clearly, the actors didn't tell the complete story that enables us to be saved. As Paul wrote to the Corinthians, "If Christ has not been raised, *your faith* is worthless; you are still in your sins" (1 Corinthians 15:17, emphasis added).

What would you say to people who claim to be Christians but who do not believe that Jesus came back to life?

RESPONDING TO "THE FAITH"

Understandably, when the followers of Jesus Christ began to proclaim this resurrection message, many of the Jewish leaders denied what was being taught. However, there were many of the priests who realized they had made a serious mistake in rejecting Jesus as the Messiah. They could not continue to deny the facts. They understood that David's prophecy in Psalm 16 referred to the resurrected Christ who had appeared to Peter, to the other apostles and to a number of other men and women who had been Christ's disciples (see Acts 2:25-28). Luke recorded the following in the book of Acts:

> So the preaching about God flourished, the number of the disciples in Jerusalem multiplied greatly, and *a large group of priests* became obedient to *the faith* (Acts 6:7, emphasis added).

Here, Luke used the phrase "the faith" to refer to what these Jewish leaders came to believe about Jesus Christ. He was and is the promised Messiah, who was crucified, buried, rose from the grave and ascended to heaven and will come again just as He said He would.

PAUL'S CONVERSION

Paul's personal testimony is one of the greatest conversion stories in Christian history. Before he became a believer, he was well known as a persecutor of Christ's disciples. In fact, after Stephen proclaimed God's redemptive plan before the Jewish leaders in Jerusalem—beginning with Abraham's story—Paul [then called Saul] approved of his death by stoning (see Acts 7:1-60).

This was just the beginning of Paul's murderous activities (see Acts 8:1-3). But God had another plan. While Paul was on the way to Damascus to capture the Jews who believed Jesus was the Messiah, the Savior spoke to him from heaven (see Acts 9:4-5). Paul wrote about his personal encounter with Jesus in his letter to the Galatians, reporting that believers everywhere were talking about his conversion experience. They were saying, "He who formerly persecuted us now preaches *the faith* he once tried to destroy" (Galatians 1:23, emphasis added). Again, this phrase, "the faith" refers to the gospel message regarding the death, burial and resurrection of Jesus Christ.

When Jude wrote his little letter that appears in our Bibles just before the book of Revelation, he helps us understand Paul's challenge to Timothy and to all of us today:

I found it necessary to write and exhort you to contend for *the faith* that was delivered to the saints [all Christians] once for all (Jude 1:3, emphasis added).

If someone asked you to share what you believe as a Christian, what would you say?

> ## PRINCIPLE TO LIVE BY
> ## WHAT WE BELIEVE
>
> To be an example in faith, you must understand and believe the basic teachings in the New Testament about Jesus Christ.

BASIC TEACHINGS OF THE CHRISTIAN FAITH

There are a number of biblical truths that God wants us to understand and apply in our lives. However, here are some basic teachings that are foundational in explaining "the faith." These truths are stated simply but carefully, and they reflect what Timothy believed and taught:

- God is three persons—Father, Son and Holy Spirit—yet one God.
- God the Father sent His Son, Jesus Christ, to die for the sins of all people.
- Jesus Christ was God who came in human flesh and lived a sinless life so that He could be the perfect sacrifice for our sins.
- Jesus, as the perfect sacrifice for our sins, chose to die and to pay the penalty for the sins of all people.
- Jesus Christ rose from the grave and made it possible for us to have eternal life, in the present and for all eternity.
- When Jesus Christ returned to heaven, God sent the Holy Spirit to indwell all who receive the gift of eternal life because of Christ's death and resurrection.
- We can only be saved when by grace through faith we receive this free gift of eternal life.
- Once we've received the gift of eternal life, we are able to live more and more like Jesus Christ if we follow the leading of the indwelling Holy Spirit.

WHO IS JESUS CHRIST?

In the last chapter, we pointed out that without Jesus Christ, biblical Christianity falls apart. This is true because He is the resurrected and living Christ. All other religious leaders developed and taught what they believe was a "way to live," but they were not in themselves "the way, the truth, and the life" (John 14:6). When these leaders died, they did not come back to life. Jesus Christ did! Furthermore, He always existed in the "form of God" even before He came to earth (Philippians 2:6)!

A DRAMATIC STORY (JOHN 9)

There is a wonderful story in John's Gospel about a man who was blind from birth. Jesus put mud on his eyes and told him to go and wash in the pool of Siloam. When he did, he was miraculously healed.

When he returned from the pool, he met his neighbors whom he could see for the first time. They were astonished and asked him what had happened. He simply explained that a "*man* called Jesus" had healed him (John 9:11, emphasis added).

Later, the Pharisees asked him what he had to say about this Jesus who he said had healed him. This was a different question. Beginning to think more deeply, he answered that he thought Jesus must be "a *prophet!*" (v. 17, emphasis added).

This was not what the Pharisees wanted to hear. They rejected his answer, actually accusing him of lying about being blind. However, when they contacted the man's parents, they verified that he was their son and that he had indeed been born blind. Consequently, the Pharisees asked the man to explain what had happened. And once again, he told them his story. But when he heard these religious leaders say that they didn't believe Jesus was from God, he blurted out, "If this man were not *from God*, He wouldn't be able to do anything" (v. 33, emphasis added).

At this point, these religious leaders were so angry they literally threw this man out of the temple. It was then that Jesus found him and asked, "Do you believe in the Son of Man?" (v. 35). Being able to see Jesus for the first time, he cried out, "I believe, Lord!" (v. 38). He then demonstrated his belief by worshiping Jesus Christ!

This is indeed a fascinating and dramatic story. You can see the man's faith develop:

- First, he believed Jesus was *a man*!
- Second, he believed Jesus was *a prophet*!
- Third, he believed Jesus was *from* God!
- Fourth, he believed Jesus *was God*, which was demonstrated by his worship!

Again, we'd like to ask you the question! *Who do you believe Jesus is?* There are those who believe that He was a good man, a great teacher and even a great prophet. He, of course, was all of these. However, how could He be this kind of man if He claimed to be God unless He *was* God?

C. S. Lewis was also a "blind man"—spiritually, that is. In fact, he claimed to be an atheist. But then he began to study carefully what Jesus taught about Himself. He finally concluded that if a man claimed to be God and is not God, he would either be crazy or a great deceiver. Certainly, he would not be a good man or a trustworthy teacher and prophet. Like the blind man in Jerusalem, Lewis came to believe that Jesus was who He claimed to be—God who became a man. You see, this is why the true message of Christianity in the Bible is dependent on Jesus! If we remove Jesus from this divine story, it is no longer the Christian story!

So, who do you believe Jesus is? Your answer has eternal implications. John recorded these implications when he wrote these words:

The one who believes in the Son has eternal life, but the one who refuses to believe in the Son will not see life; instead, the wrath of God remains on him (John 3:36).

In this chapter, we've written about "the faith." This refers to what Christians believe, regardless of their church or denominational affiliation. Central to this belief is that Jesus Christ came from God, was God and lived a perfect life. He died on the cross for our sins, rose again and ascended once again to be with God the Father. He then sent the Holy Spirit to dwell in the hearts of all true believers. Someday, Jesus will come again to take all true believers to be with Him forever.

Are you one of those who believe that Jesus is the Christ, the Son of God? If you do, you have eternal life!

A QUESTION FOR DISCUSSION

Why is it illogical and even irrational to believe that Jesus Christ was a good man and a great teacher and yet not believe His claims to be God?

18

Practicing Living Faith

PRINCIPLE TO LIVE BY

To be an example in faith, you must draw on God's power through the Holy Spirit and, at the same time, determine to avoid any sinful attitudes and actions that will keep you from focusing on the Lord Jesus Christ.

On one occasion, I (Gene) remember listening to a well-known Christian leader, Dr. Francis Schaeffer. He was delivering a powerful message. He's now in heaven, but his influence continues on in my life. I still remember a question he asked that really made me stop and think:

If you removed every reference from the Bible to *having faith*, would it really make any difference in the way you live your life as a Christian?

That was and is a convicting question. Do you know why? In our culture, our tendency is to do things ourselves. We're often taught that whatever our mind can conceive and believe, we can achieve! And, when people use the word "believe" in this way, they simply mean "have faith in yourself"! In other words, we really don't need God's help. We can do anything!

I must confess that even as a Christian I often tend to try to achieve my goals and solve my problems with my own wisdom and skills. I really don't rely on the Lord as I should. Followers of Jesus Christ in New Testament times understood much more clearly what it means to live by faith than we do! They were often persecuted. Sometimes they didn't know where their next meal was coming from. They were often scorned and ignored. They *had* to trust God to survive. This is also true of many people today who live in other parts of the world.

When Paul was in prison, he set a great example when he wrote to the Philippians and told them he didn't know whether he was going to live or die. However, he demonstrated remarkable faith when he said, "For me, living is Christ and dying is gain" (Philippians 1:21).

Don't misunderstand! It's not wrong to have the security and opportunities that we do to meet our needs, to accumulate things, to achieve our personal goals. In fact, Paul exhorted some of the Thessalonians who were lazy that "if anyone isn't willing to work, he should not eat" (2 Thessalonians 3:10).

The Lord honors human diligence. My challenge is to never forget, not for even a moment, that I need God and that I need to trust Him from day to day with everything. What about you?

As you live from day to day, how often do you stop and think about God's presence and power in your life?

MEANWHILE, BACK IN EPHESUS!

Again imagine sitting with a group of Christians in a "house church" in Ephesus. Many of those who have gathered are having a very difficult time. Some have changed vocations and have financial needs. Two men who had been selling silver shrines of Artemis, the fertility goddess they had formerly worshiped in the pagan temple, no longer did this as a livelihood. Some had stopped making a living by dabbling in satanic worship and telling fortunes. Others were being shunned by their neighbors because of their faith in Christ, and still others were being persecuted by the politicians in the city.

Timothy would have been well aware of these personal needs. To encourage these believers, he once again carefully unrolled the letter to the Ephesians and read from Paul's prayer:

> For this reason I bow my knees before the Father from whom every family in heaven and on earth is named. [I pray] that He may grant you, according to the riches of His glory, *to be strengthened with power through His Spirit* in the inner man, and *that the Messiah may dwell in your hearts through faith* (Ephesians 3:14-17a, emphasis added).

This is one of the most powerful and helpful prayers in the New Testament to help us develop our *living faith*, no matter our circumstances or where we live. Even though Paul initially prayed this prayer for the Ephesians, you can pray this same prayer for yourself and for others.

GOD THE SON

Look more carefully at this prayer as it relates to how you can live by faith at this very moment in your life. Paul prayed that Jesus, the Messiah, might dwell in the hearts of these Ephesian Christians *through faith*.

How is that possible? After Jesus' resurrection, he had a physical body, and the disciples recognized Him and touched Him. The apostles saw Him "taken up as they were watching, and a cloud received Him out of their sight" (Acts 1:9). In fact, Paul reminded Timothy in the very letter we've been studying that "there is one God and one mediator between God and man, *a man*, Christ Jesus" (1 Timothy 2:5, emphasis added).

In other words, somewhere in this vast universe, Jesus in His glorified and resurrected body is representing all of His children to God the Father. If you have experienced saving faith, Jesus is your "great high priest who has passed through the heavens" (Hebrews 4:14). He sympathizes with all of your weaknesses and offers His mercy and grace when you pray (see vv. 14-16).

Often when we share the salvation message, we encourage people "to invite Jesus into their hearts." Little children particularly have some very distorted thoughts about this statement since it understandably doesn't seem to make sense. They can only visualize Jesus from what they've seen in pictures. Even adults with little biblical background get confused. How can a man—in this case, *one perfect man*—dwell in the hearts of every Christian and yet be with God in heaven?

GOD THE HOLY SPIRIT

Paul answered this question in the earlier part of his prayer in Ephesians 3:16: "[I pray] that He [God the Father] may grant you, according to the riches of His glory, to be strengthened with power *through His Spirit* in the inner man" (emphasis added). The answer to Christ's presence in our hearts is through the person of the Holy Spirit.

When Jesus told His disciples shortly before His death that He was going away to prepare a place for them (see John 14:2), He also promised that He would ask God the Father to send the Holy Spirit to be with them forever (see John 14:15-16). When the Day of Pentecost came, this promise was fulfilled in the hearts of those who witnessed the Holy Spirit's coming. At that time, the apostle Peter reminded everyone in Jerusalem of Jesus' promise—that the Holy Spirit was not only a gift to the apostles but to everyone, "as many as the Lord our God will call" (Acts 2:39).

Though the Holy Spirit manifests His presence in various ways at different times and in different situations, one thing is certain: When we receive the Lord Jesus Christ as our personal Savior, the Holy Spirit comes to dwell in our hearts. We may not even be conscious of His presence, but He is there. You see, the Spirit of God is Christ in us—as Paul wrote to the Colossians (see Colossians 1:27).

DAILY STRENGTH AND POWER

Look even more carefully at Paul's prayer. If Christ, through the Holy Spirit, is in our hearts when we receive Him by faith, why did He pray for the Ephesians that Christ "may dwell in your hearts *through faith*" (Ephesians 3:17, emphasis added)?

Again, Paul answered this question when he referred to being "strengthened with power through His Spirit in the inner man [our hearts]." To experience "saving faith" is a supernatural experience. Just so, "living by faith" is a supernatural experience. Paul was praying that these believers in Ephesus might experience God's presence and power moment by moment in their lives. This would happen if they continued to *live by faith*.

In explaining this great truth, perhaps Timothy continued to unroll this marvelous scroll until he came to the end of the letter and read these words:

> Finally, be strengthened by the Lord and by His vast strength. Put on the full armor of God so that you can stand against the tactics of the Devil (Ephesians 6:10-11).

Here, Paul used an illustration of a Roman soldier who goes into battle with his armor on. As Paul illustrated each piece of armor with a spiritual truth, he described "living faith" when he wrote:

> In every situation take the *shield of faith*, and with it you will be able to extinguish the flaming arrows of the evil one (Ephesians 6:16, emphasis added).

RUNNING A RACE

Living the Christian life by faith is indeed a supernatural experience. However, it also involves human responsibility and personal discipline. God does not force us to trust Him. Rather, He has given us the freedom to make choices; and when we make the right choices, God will help us live in His perfect will.

To illustrate this truth, the author of Hebrews used the metaphor of an athletic event: running in a race. We don't know who wrote this letter, but Timothy knew the author of this letter personally since he is mentioned in the benediction and farewell. Later in his life, probably after Paul's death at the hands of the Roman Emperor, Timothy was also imprisoned for his faith in Jesus Christ. However, when the author—unknown to us—had completed this letter to the Hebrews, Timothy had just been released from prison and was going to travel with the author to some unidentified location (see Hebrews 13:23). No longer a young man, Timothy was still living by faith and running the race victoriously! What a wonderful example to all of us!

Take a careful look at this athletic race illustration. The runners are in a huge stadium, surrounded by a large crowd of people who were cheering them on. Notice how the illustration and the application to our Christian lives overlap:

> Therefore since we also have such a *large cloud of witnesses* surrounding us, let us *lay aside every weight and the sin* that so easily ensnares us, and run with endurance the race that lies before us, *keeping our eyes on Jesus, the source and perfecter of our faith*, who for the joy that lay before Him endured a cross and despised the shame, and has sat down at the right hand of God's throne (Hebrews 12:1-2, emphasis added).

Lay Aside Every Weight

When athletes participated in these Roman games, they discarded every piece of clothing that would keep them from running fast. This applies to any sin in our lives that keeps us from running our spiritual race victoriously and in God's perfect will.

Keep Our Eyes on Jesus

The athletes also kept their eyes on the goal. They didn't look to the right or the left. Just so, Jesus Christ is our goal. He set the example. He ran the race victoriously and, with His help, so can we!

A Large Cloud of Witnesses

Who were those who formed this "large crowd of witnesses"? They probably were the men and women who are described in the previous paragraphs (see Hebrews 11:4-38). They were people who *lived by faith*—Old Testament believers like Abel, Enoch, Noah, Abraham and his wife, Sarah, and their son, Isaac. We also meet Joseph and Moses, and Rahab who had been a prostitute in Jericho. There are others mentioned, though not by name, many who lived in Timothy's era but who had been killed because of their witness for Jesus Christ. At the end of this list we read:

> All these were approved *through their faith* (Hebrews 11:39a, emphasis added).

A REAL-LIFE EXPERIENCE

On one occasion, my wife and I (Gene) stood in one of these stadiums in what is now modern Turkey. It still stands in a 360-degree configuration. As I sat on one of the stone seats and looked at this amazing structure, I reflected on this paragraph in Hebrews. In my mind's eye, I could see this "large crowd of witnesses" seated in this huge circle. I could envision runners down on the field, charging toward the goal.

This seems to be the picture in the mind of the biblical author of Hebrews. Nearly 2,000 years ago it was a real-life experience for him and even Timothy. Perhaps they sat in a similar stadium together actually watching a footrace. They noticed that all runners had removed any article of clothing that would slow them down. This reminded them of the sins that we commit that keep us from running our spiritual race effectively.

The author of this letter also noticed how all of the runners kept their eyes fixed on the goal. Consequently, they thought about Jesus Christ and His perfect life. That should always be *our goal*. He is "the source and perfecter of our faith" (Hebrews 12:2).

PRINCIPLE TO LIVE BY
LIVING BY FAITH

To be an example in faith, you must draw on God's power through the Holy Spirit and, at the same time, determine to avoid any sinful attitudes and actions that will keep you from focusing on the Lord Jesus Christ.

WHAT IS LIVING FAITH?

I (Kenton) would like to address a very important misconception. Some people believe that "living by faith" is a leap in the dark. Some call it "blind faith." Not true! Note what the author of Hebrews wrote leading up to what we sometimes call the Hall of Faith:

Now faith is the reality of what is hoped for, the proof of what is not seen (Hebrews 11:1).

True, this may appear to be blind faith—or what some people call "faith in faith." Or, "faith without facts"! The facts are that God has never operated that way. He has not asked us to believe something that has not been verified. He has not asked us to believe something that is irrational and lacks historical fact.

To help make this point, let me share an experience I had when I was living in Colorado and was a member of an alpine ski team. Several of the team members and I went to compete in a downhill race in Northwest Montana. On the day of the race it was so foggy on the top of the mountain that you couldn't see the first gate. Furthermore, you couldn't see the second gate until *after* you skied through the first gate. Yet, when *my time* to race came, I had to leave the starting gate and throw myself down the mountain, navigating the course at speeds up to 70 and 80 miles per hour.

The fact is, I knew where I was headed even though I couldn't see what lay ahead. I had surveyed the slope *and* memorized the course—visualizing every turn and the placement of every gate. In my mind's eye, I could see what lay ahead. Also, members of the race committee spread pine boughs on the course so the racers could see the contour of the slope and its many variations. When I left the top of the mountain, it was definitely not blind faith—even though I couldn't see exactly where I was headed.

There was another dimension to my faith as I left the starting gate. I trusted my training to help me negotiate the turns. I prepared my equipment by sharpening the edges and adjusting the bindings. I waxed the base of the skis so they would respond to my movements through the high-speed turns down the course. I had to rely on my training and preparation, and then I had to put those skills to the test by racing.

A HUMAN PERSPECTIVE

From a human point of view at least, my downhill racing experience illustrates that faith in the message of the Bible concerning Jesus Christ is not based on blind faith. Nearly 40 men of varied backgrounds recorded the Scriptures over a 1,500-year period. And yet their message is consistent. What they wrote contains hundreds of fulfilled prophecies. Their historical and geographical references have been verified again and again by archaeological discoveries—which are still happening today. If you stop and think for a moment, you'll conclude, as we have, that it actually takes more faith to believe that the Bible is merely human in its origin than to believe that God has inspired it. The fact is that there is an incredible amount of evidence to verify that the Bible is true. People who reject this reality normally have little knowledge of the history of the Bible and what it says.

Following through on my skiing illustration, when you leave the starting gate in your spiritual race, be assured that you are not living by blind faith. The course has been clearly marked out for you in the Bible, which is a very trustworthy record of God's will for your life. Furthermore, the more you discipline yourself to live a godly life, the more confident you will be that you're on the right course.

A DIVINE PERSPECTIVE

There is another dimension to Christian faith. It's based on the supernatural. The Holy Spirit enables people to believe in and trust what God has said. This is part of the divine mystery that we see throughout the story of the Bible—a marvelous blending of the human and the divine. Even so, the story of the Bible in itself helps verify this marvelous balance in our lives.

Here is a very important lesson! Don't allow people—even very educated people—to destroy your faith in the reliability of the biblical message. Many people who try have a very limited view of both the total message of the Bible and how it came into existence. Furthermore, if they do not know the Author of the Bible personally, they will have difficulty both understanding and accepting its message.

In terms of living by faith daily, what I've just shared is foundational and helpful; but simply trusting God from day to day enables us to experience God's guidance.

TWO LIFE VERSES

I've often heard my dad share that two of his life verses are found in Proverbs:

> Trust in the LORD with all your heart, and do not rely on your own understanding; think about Him in all your ways, and He will guide you on the right paths (Proverbs 3:5-6).

These verses are also very reassuring to me. What God says in these proverbs is foundational to being able to live by faith. As you meditate on these verses, answer the following questions:

- What does it mean to "trust in the Lord with all your heart"?
- What does it mean to "not rely on your own understanding"?

- What does it mean to "think about Him in all your ways"?
- What is God's promise when you "live by faith" and practice these biblical exhortations?

UNIT 7

Maintain Moral Purity

No one should despise your youth; instead you should be an example to the
believers in speech, in conduct, in love, in faith, in purity.
1 TIMOTHY 4:12

Timothy lived in a world where most people persistently violated God's will
regarding sexual purity. Fortunately, Timothy's mother—a God-fearing
Jew—had taught him the Old Testament Scriptures from childhood. However, this did not protect him from being exposed to the immorality in the
Roman city of Lystra where he grew up.

Today, you live in a world that is becoming more and more like the
world Timothy lived in. The good news is that as a Christ-follower, you
have God's Word to guide you. Through a personal relationship with the
Lord Jesus Christ and the power of the indwelling Holy Spirit, you can live
more and more in God's will in all aspects of your life, including being
morally pure. It is possible! Though tempted like all young men, Timothy
demonstrated this in his own life. The following chapters will help you become this kind of young man, along with three principles to live by.

19

Discovering God's Moral Standard

PRINCIPLE TO LIVE BY

To walk in God's will, you must be committed to living according to a biblical moral standard.

I (Gene) grew up as a country boy living on a farm in Indiana. My older cousins lived close by on another farm, and when I was old enough, we played together regularly.

The oldest boy was definitely a bad influence. In fact, even as a very young child (at ages three and four) I remember listening to him tell dirty stories and saw him shamelessly engage in immoral behavior. If I stop to think about it, those are impressions that I can conjure up in my mind even to this day. Unfortunately, this cousin continued this behavior until he died as an alcoholic before he reached the age of 50. His life was a tragic story.

My parents moved to another farm when I was six years old. Fortunately, this cousin's influence was gone. But there were others—such as a fourth-grade kid who liked to share cartoon pornography with his classmates that he had received from his older brother. Again, to this day, if I stop and think, I can recall those images that were imprinted on my impressionable nine-year-old mind.

As I grew up and entered junior high school, I again encountered classmates who regularly shared dirty jokes and talked about their sexual exploits. Yes, I was tempted to participate in their lifestyle, but I thank God He protected me until, at age 16, I put my faith in Jesus Christ and became a born-again Christian. This moment in my life started me on a whole new journey as I began to renew my mind with the Word of God and not "be conformed" to this world but "be transformed" (Romans 12:1-2).

Eventually, I attended a Bible college and met a wonderful girl. We later married, and how thankful I am that both of us were virgins. As a Christian couple, we could now engage in a sexual relationship free from guilt and enjoy this sacred gift with each other as God intended.

TIMOTHY'S EARLY YEARS

In contrast to my country background, Timothy grew up as a city boy. We can be sure that most of the children he played with in Lystra acted out what they had learned from their family members, their neighbors and even from the priests in the temple of Zeus. Timothy, of course, grew up never reading dirty books and looking at pornography, never seeing sex on television or in movies and never logging onto the Internet to view sensuous sites. However, he heard about and witnessed explicit sexual activities that violated God's laws in unimaginable ways. Various forms of decadent immorality were everywhere!

Thankfully, Timothy had a God-fearing Jewish mother who taught him moral values from the Old Testament. We can be certain she taught him the seventh Commandment, "Do not commit adultery" (Exodus 20:14). However, we can also assume that his unbelieving Gentile father violated this commandment regularly. Engaging in sexual activity with women other than their wives was common behavior among pagan men in the Roman Empire.

BECOMING A CHRIST-FOLLOWER

Timothy became a Christian when the apostle Paul came to Lystra on his first missionary journey. After his decision to receive the Lord Jesus as his personal Savior, Timothy's life began to change. In fact, when Paul returned on his second journey several years later, he heard that Timothy had become a dedicated disciple of Jesus. Knowing Paul, he would have sat down with this young man in a personal and private setting and, as his spiritual father, talked about God's plan for sexual purity. Though Paul had not yet written his first letter to the Thessalonians, his conversation would certainly have reflected on the same basic instructions he later wrote to these believers:

> For this is God's will, your *sanctification: that you abstain from sexual immorality*, so that each of you knows how to possess his own vessel in *sanctification* and honor, not with lustful desires, like the Gentiles who don't know God (1 Thessalonians 4:3-5, emphasis added).

The word "sanctification" means "holiness." When we are saved by faith, we are *sanctified*. No matter what our past, present or future sins, God sees us as *absolutely holy* because of Jesus' *perfect sacrifice* on the cross. But once we experience "saving faith," God wants us to live a holy and godly life.

A LIFETIME CHALLENGE

Living a holy life is a lifetime process. As long as we are living on this earth, we must be on guard against yielding to sexual temptation. However, regardless of our experiences growing up, we can "*be transformed by the renewing of [our] mind*, so that [we] may discern what is the good, pleasing, and perfect will of God" (Romans 12:2, emphasis added).

This process of becoming like Christ will someday be complete in us, but not until we are with Jesus in heaven. We will then experience the reality that God already sees because He is omniscient, or all-knowing. As John wrote, "We will be like Him, because we will see Him as He is" (1 John 3:2b).

In the meantime, we live in the here and now, and living a sexually pure life should be a part of this process. This is what Paul was referring to when he also wrote in his letter to the Thessalonians: "For God has not called us to impurity, but to sanctification"—which means learning to live a holy life (1 Thessalonians 4:7).

Do you have a mature Christian man with whom you can talk about God's plan for sex and relationships?

TRAVELING EXPERIENCES

When Timothy became a missionary and traveled to various cities in the Roman Empire, he often heard Paul teach about God's plan for sexual purity—both before marriage and during marriage. For example, when the team arrived in Corinth—one of the most immoral cities in the Roman Empire—Timothy not only heard messages on God's plan for sexual purity, but he had certainly read the letter Paul wrote to the Roman Christians from this pagan city. In fact, at the end of that letter, Paul actually sent greetings *from* Timothy, who probably reviewed what Paul had written (see Romans 16:21). In the opening paragraphs, Paul was *very* specific in describing various sexual sins:

- Heterosexual immorality between men and women: "Therefore God delivered them over in the cravings of their hearts to sexual impurity, so that their bodies were degraded among themselves" (Romans 1:24).

- Homosexuality: "This is why God delivered them over to degrading passions. For even their females exchanged natural sexual intercourse for what is unnatural. The males in the same way also left natural sexual intercourse with females and were inflamed in their lust for one another. Males committed shameless acts with males and received in their own persons the appropriate penalty for their perversion" (Romans 1:26-27).

What Paul described in this letter was not new to Timothy. As a young man growing up in the culture of the Roman Empire, he had been exposed to these sins right in his home city of Lystra. And when Paul wrote this letter from Corinth, this kind of immorality was everywhere in this pagan city. In fact, sexual degradation existed *wherever* Paul's missionary team traveled to proclaim the good news that Jesus Christ has come to die for all of our sins—including sexual sins—and to transform our lives.

Because you live in a world where sex is frequently used to sell products, stimulate sexual appetites and entertain with risqué scenes, what can you do to avoid sexual temptations?

When Paul later sent Timothy to Corinth to remind them of his "ways in Christ Jesus" (1 Corinthians 4:17), we can be sure this young man often read from Paul's letter to the Corinthian church, explaining God's will for their lives. For example, visualize the scene as Timothy would have reviewed Paul's instructions in what we identify as chapter 6 in 1 Corinthians:

Do not be deceived: no sexually immoral people, idolaters, adulterers, male prostitutes, homosexuals, thieves, greedy people, drunkards, revilers, or swindlers will inherit God's kingdom. *Some of you were like this;* but you were *washed,* you were *sanctified,* you were *justified* in the name of the Lord Jesus Christ and by the Spirit of our God (1 Corinthians 6:9b-11, emphasis added).

Needless to say, it took time for many of the Corinthian believers to begin to live pure lives. But because many of these pagan people were spiritually born again, they were able, with God's strength, to begin to manifest the fruit of the Holy Spirit rather than continuing to manifest the works of the flesh, such as sexual immorality, moral impurity and promiscuity (see Galatians 5:19,22). This miraculous change is what Paul was referring to when he wrote in his second letter to the Corinthians:

Therefore if anyone is in Christ, there is a *new creation*; old things have passed away, and look, *new things have come* (2 Corinthians 5:17, emphasis added).

PRINCIPLE TO LIVE BY
A BIBLICAL COMMITMENT

To walk in God's will, you must be committed to living according to a biblical moral standard.

PURITY ... WHAT DOES PAUL MEAN?

Paul put a final exclamation point on the list of character qualities Timothy was to model by calling Timothy to live a "pure" life. What does this actually mean? How do you live a "pure" life? What does that look like?

As "Pure as the Driven Snow"

As I reflect on the concept of "purity," I (Kenton) can't help but recall a mental picture of being in the mountains in the dead of winter. I have gone heli-skiing several times, and one of my favorite parts of the trip is to get dropped off by a helicopter in the Canadian backcountry, right at tree line. On this particular run, I had to carry the emergency avalanche backpack, which means I had to go last. The others in my group headed down the mountain, skiing through trackless powder. As I watched them disappear over a ridge in the slope, I was alone, standing in the middle of gigantic pine trees that are hundreds of years old. They were towering over my head, reaching toward the sky. As I glanced behind me, I saw mountain peaks covered with snow, standing majestically, displaying their strength.

On that day it was snowing, but the wind was calm. The snowflakes were as large as quarters. They fell to the earth, settling on the pine branches, or found their resting place on the snow-covered ground. As I stood in the middle of this wilderness, my ears buzzed in the silence. Straining to listen, I imagined I heard the snow drifting through the air. All my senses were awakening to the clean, unblemished, innocent and natural setting.

I was in the middle of a pristine playground, pure and unmarked by mankind. The freshly fallen snow was untouched. It was a white blanket stretching endlessly as far as my eyes could see. This smooth canopy covered the imperfections in the ground and concealed every blemish and stain that existed before the snowfall. It filled in all the holes, crevasses and cracks on the mountainside. Nature stood as a testament to God's strength, beauty, creativity, grace—and holiness!

I was captivated by the moment. I didn't want to move. I just wanted to stay and admire God's handiwork. I became distinctly aware of God's presence in my life. I was not alone on the mountain. God was right there with me. He made it possible for me to enter into His presence and share this moment with Him. I was humbled that the Creator of the universe wants a relationship with me.

As I reflect on that experience, I'm reminded that our lives are not unlike the earth when it is covered by snow. Our lives are not smooth and pure. There are holes, crevasses and cracks representing the sin and pain in our lives that need healing and covering. No matter how hard we try to make things better, we can't fill in the cracks that scar our lives. To cover over our sins and heal our hurts, it takes something outside of us—a Source that is greater than anything we can accomplish on our own.

For me, the fresh snow falling to the ground that day represented God's grace. He causes the snow to fall. He fills in the holes in our souls. He covers and heals the scars of our past. He makes our lives whole. He does this all on His own. He does this because He loves us. He restores our purity. Remember that when we accept Jesus as our Savior, He makes us a new creation and presents us as holy and pure before God.

"Whiter than Snow"

Thankfully, as a young man, you can't identify with the depth of David's sexual sin that he committed with Bathsheba—another man's wife. However, all of us can identify with the need for forgiveness in some area of our lives. For you, it may include some form of immorality, if not in actions, in your thoughts. The good news is that God forgives all sins when we sincerely repent. Note David's heartfelt prayer for forgiveness:

> Be gracious to me, God, according to Your faithful love; according to Your abundant compassion, blot out my rebellion. Wash away my guilt, and cleanse me from my sin. . . . Purify me with hyssop, and I will be clean; wash me, and I will be *whiter than snow* (Psalm 51:1-2,7, emphasis added).

David had seen the beautiful, newly fallen snow on Mount Hermon, the only place in the land of Israel where this happens regularly. Like me, he was reminded of what it means to be pure in God's sight. The prophet Isaiah was also impressed with this metaphor. Note what he wrote:

"Come, let us discuss this," says the LORD. "Though your sins are like scarlet, they will be as *white as snow*; though they are as red as crimson, they will be like wool" (Isaiah 1:18, emphasis added).

GOD'S GRACE IS SUFFICIENT FOR YOU

No matter what you and I have done or will do, we rest assured that God's grace is sufficient to cover our sins and heal our hurts. When He calls us to be examples in purity, He doesn't expect us to be perfect, because no one is perfect, except for Jesus. God wants us to be moving toward Him and living a life that is chaste, free from sin, innocent and pure.

I don't know where you are in following God's plan regarding your sexuality; what you allow your mind to dwell on, what you allow yourself to look at, how you interact with other people. If you are struggling to maintain purity in this area of your life, let me encourage you. There is hope, and we will look at some practical things in the last two chapters that you can do that will help you. I encourage you to do these things:

- Reflect again on my illustration regarding the newly fallen snow.
- Read David's entire prayer in Psalm 51.
- Ask God to help you live a pure life, even though many people around you are violating God's will for their lives.
- Memorize 1 John 1:9: "If we confess our sins, He is faithful and righteous to forgive us our sins and to cleanse us from all unrighteousness."

20

Living by God's Moral Standard

PRINCIPLE TO LIVE BY

To live a life of moral purity, you must flee from sexual temptations that will lead you to make decisions that are a violation of God's will.

Today we live in a world where sexual values have changed dramatically. Many young people your age no longer believe that sex is reserved only for a man and woman who are married. They've been taught that this is an old-fashioned idea. In some situations, young children are being taught that gay and lesbian relationships are normal for those who have these desires. Even some religious leaders who claim to be Christians are teaching that the sexual standards in the Bible that we looked at in chapter 19 are old-fashioned and not meant for today.

To illustrate this reality, when was the last time you saw a Hollywood movie that promotes sexual abstinence before marriage? There are very few, if any. The story line often features casual sex—sometimes with a variety of partners. Even stories of serious romance promote premarital sex. In other words, if you "love someone," sex is a natural prelude to eventually saying "I do!"

PAUL'S CHALLENGE TO TIMOTHY

Paul challenged Timothy to always treat "younger women as sisters" (1 Timothy 5:1-2). Just as he would never engage in an incestuous relationship with his own sister, he was to relate to all young women with "all propriety"—which means "in all purity."

What precautions do you take to keep yourself sexually pure?

As a young single man, Timothy was to be on guard at all times. Many of these young women had also lived immoral lives before they became Christians. Consequently, they too could be tempted to seduce Timothy. After all, he *was* single! Later in this same letter, Paul cautioned him, "Don't share in the sins of others. *Keep yourself pure*" (1 Timothy 5:22b, emphasis added).

A Powerful Example

As Paul and Timothy traveled together on their various missionary journeys and observed the pagan sexual practices throughout the Roman Empire, they certainly reflected together on the story of Joseph. This young man was just 17 or 18 years old when his brothers sold him as a slave.

When he was put on the auction block in Egypt, a high-ranking official named Potiphar bought him. Because of Joseph's diligence and faithfulness, as well as God's blessing on his life, Potiphar eventually put him in charge of his whole household. This was a powerful position for a young man.

It was then Joseph faced one of his greatest temptations. Potiphar's wife tried to seduce him. In fact, she tried day after day, but with no success. Joseph told her he would not violate her husband's trust. More importantly, he would not violate God's moral laws.

One day, Potiphar's wife grabbed Joseph and tried to force him to commit adultery. Joseph turned and ran. When he rejected her seductive actions, her sexual passion quickly turned to anger and she falsely accused him of trying to rape her. Even though Joseph ended up in prison, he had obeyed God rather than committing this horrible sin. He paid a difficult price, but ultimately God blessed him for his commitment to moral purity (see Genesis 39:1-23).

When Paul penned his second and final letter to Timothy, he may have alluded to Joseph's sterling example when he wrote:

> Flee from *youthful passions*, and pursue righteousness, faith, love, and peace, along with those who call on the Lord from a *pure heart* (2 Timothy 2:22, emphasis added).

A Lesson from David

As Paul and Timothy observed sexual immorality, even among the Jewish people who lived in these pagan Roman cities, they certainly must have reflected on King David's moral failure. Paul would have reminded Timothy that David's moral failure was not the *temptation*. It was the steps he took that led to his immoral act:

1. First, he saw Bathsheba bathing—"a very beautiful woman" (2 Samuel 11:2b).
2. Second, he "sent someone to inquire about her" (2 Samuel 11:3a).

3. Third, he "sent messengers to get her" (2 Samuel 11:4a).
4. Fourth, "he slept with her" (2 Samuel 11:4b).

Perhaps Paul explained it this way:

You see, Timothy, David did not sin when he was tempted. He responded as any man would when he happened to see such a beautiful woman. However, he didn't turn away and flee from the situation. Rather, his temptation led to sin when he purposely kept looking, eventually inquired about her and then made a decision to have her come to his quarters so that he could engage in a sexual relationship.

Timothy, this is what Jesus meant when he taught that "everyone who looks at a woman to lust for her has already committed adultery with her in his heart" (Matthew 5:28). Again, to be tempted is not sin. But temptation can quickly lead to sin—even in our hearts—when we decide to violate God's will and then take steps to make it happen.

When Paul wrote to the Corinthians, he addressed the subject of temptation and wrote some very realistic but encouraging words:

No temptation has overtaken you except what is common to humanity. God is faithful and He will not allow you to be tempted beyond what you are able, but with the temptation He will also provide a way of escape, so that you are able to bear it (1 Corinthians 10:13).

---

*What steps do you need to take to keep temptation
from becoming sinful thoughts and actions?*

> ## PRINCIPLE TO LIVE BY
> ## GOD'S MORAL STANDARD
>
> **To live a life of moral purity, you must flee from sexual temptations that will lead you to make decisions that are a violation of God's will.**

SATAN'S TACTICS

Satan works incredibly hard to take God's sacred gift of sex and twist our thinking about it. We must always be on guard, since his initial tactics will not be outright war that you can easily recognize! He will work around the edges of your life, numbing your conscience. He will attempt to lead you down a sinful, compromising path one step at a time.

You may have heard the story of the frog and the kettle. Put the frog in a boiling pot of hot water and he'll immediately jump out. However, put him in cold water and heat up the kettle little by little and the heat will gradually overtake him. Then it's too late! Just so, Satan wants to gradually numb your conscience so that you don't even realize how far you are from God.

SUGGESTIONS FOR RESISTING SEXUAL TEMPTATION

The following are some suggestions for how you can be on guard against Satan's tactics and resist sexual temptation.

Seek Forgiveness for Past Failures

If you have had sexual experiences in the past that you regret, confess your sins to God and accept His forgiveness. Remember that God's grace is sufficient and His mercies "are new every morning" (Lamentations 3:23). Remember also that the apostle John wrote:

> If we confess our sins, He is faithful and righteous to forgive us our sins and to cleanse us from all unrighteousness (1 John 1:9).

Don't allow your conscience to hold you captive to the past. Just like in the mountains where the snowfall becomes an unblemished and pristine canopy that covers all imperfections on the ground, God's grace and forgiveness cover all the blemishes and imperfections in our lives.

Renew Your Mind Daily with the Word of God

God has provided you with a pathway and the strength to move toward a relationship with Him. That pathway is Scripture. As you discovered in earlier chapters, the Bible is your compass, and it will keep you on course as you journey through life. When you read God's Word and allow it to renew your mind, God will enable you to "flee" temptation. He has provided a way to escape.

Get Real with a Group of Other Young Men

No matter what your age, you need other men in your life. Scripture speaks right to the heart of this issue: "Confess your sins to one another . . . pray for one another. . . . The intense prayer of the righteous is very powerful" (James 5:16).

Part of your adventure in this life is being a member of a team. This group of other young men will help you, encourage you and speak truth to you. But they won't live your life for you. Only God can help you and give you the strength to live for Him. However, the members of your team will be with you in the trenches, and they will be cheering you on from the sidelines.

Meet with your team consistently (I suggest weekly) and be honest with them even when you don't want to. Also, make sure that your team includes an older, more mature Christian. You need someone in your group who has encountered your battles and successfully learned lessons in life. Just like Timothy needed Paul, you need an older Christian man in your life.

Set Your Boundaries and Write Them Down

Following are some specific steps to take.

1. Write down the answers to the following questions:

   - What in my life needs to go?
   - What in my life needs to increase?
   - How do I treat women on dates?
   - How do I guard my eyes and heart in today's connected and technically advanced world?
   - Do my friends encourage my morals or do they compromise my morals?

2. Write down the decisions you need to make and the actions connected to those decisions.

3. Write down the dates when you will complete your action items. Here's an example regarding your home computer:

   - Make a decision that you want to protect your mind and your eyes by setting up a filter and a tool for accountability. Available tools include Safe Eyes and Covenant Eyes. These are leading software companies in the Christian community that have designed products to protect you and your family from exposure to sexually explicit material on the Internet. Date: _____.

   - Take action by researching the tools and installing one of the programs. Date: _____.

- Other action steps should include: talking with your parents; requesting their help; deciding on how to pay for these services; and enlisting your team members to be accountability partners by getting email addresses and listing them in the software tool so they receive your Internet usage reports by mail. Date: _____.

This is just one practical but imperative suggestion. However, think about other times that you are tempted and then write down what you need to do to flee that temptation. Additional suggestions for fleeing sexual temptation include:

- Only go on double dates and group dates.
- Determine appropriate physical boundaries in your dating life and discuss them with your date.
- Be firmly committed to keeping your hands in check on dates.
- Go directly to TV channels that are appropriate to watch. Don't channel surf.
- Delete channels or block channels on your TV with risqué programming.
- Turn off the TV at night when everyone goes to bed, and read or go to bed yourself.
- Consider attending a Celebrate Recovery class in your local church to help you understand and overcome any sexual obsessions and addictions.
- Meet with a Christian counselor to help conquer habitual (addictive) sin patterns.

A FINAL CHALLENGE

A final suggestion is to memorize Philippians 4:8 and use it to evaluate what you think about. Look carefully at Paul's words to the Philippians in this verse:

Finally brothers, whatever is *true*, whatever is *honorable*, whatever is *just*, whatever is *pure*, whatever is *lovely*, whatever is *commendable*—if there is any *moral excellence* and if there is *any praise*—dwell on these things (Philippians 4:8, emphasis added).

As you think about the qualities in this verse, list the good things you think about that correspond to these qualities:

True _____
Honorable_____
Just _____
Pure _____
Lovely _____
Commendable _____
Of moral excellence _____
Worthy of praise _____

Next, look at this list of qualities once again and list those things that you think about that do not reflect these character traits.

True _____
Honorable_____
Just _____
Pure _____
Lovely _____
Commendable _____
Of moral excellence _____
Worthy of praise _____

Now that you have completed this exercise, pray specifically and ask God to help you focus on those things that help you renew your mind and heart and to eliminate those things that do not renew your mind and heart.

21

Understanding the Relationship Between Love and Sex

PRINCIPLE TO LIVE BY

To make right decisions regarding your relationship with the opposite sex, you must understand and practice three-dimensional love that is first and foremost based on God's love for you.

Meet Bill. He just turned 16. He has been dating a girl named Julie. A day ago she sent him a text message that shook him up:

Bill, I'm pregnant. I really don't know what to do. I need your help. You said you loved me when we began having sex. I really need that love now. I haven't even told my parents. Should we get married?

Today, Bill answered Julie's message:

Julie, I'm confused. I know I said I loved you, but those feelings have changed. I really don't believe we should get married. Furthermore, I'm not ready to be a "father." I think you should get an abortion.

Here's Julie's sad response:

I can't believe you don't love me anymore. You told me you loved me many times—particularly during sex and even afterwards. What happened to your feelings? Were you just telling me that because you wanted more sex? I'm devastated, and I feel all alone. How could you do this to me?

WHAT'S WRONG WITH THIS PICTURE?

Both Bill and Julie are confused. Bill doesn't understand the relationship between acting in love and responding to sexual feelings. When he told Julie he "loved her," he may have actually believed what he said. However, he was acting more on sexual desire, not understanding that true biblical love is much more than a feeling of sexual attraction.

Julie, too, is confused. She was also sexually attracted to Bill when she gave in to his desires. She actually believed he "loved her" and that she "loved him," but she didn't understand that young men can be motivated more by lustful desires than true love and that young women can also misinterpret their own feelings.

More importantly, both Bill and Julie are not committed to living by God's standard for moral purity. Not only did they violate God's will, but when they faced the result of their sin, they didn't turn to God for forgiveness. Bill didn't take responsibility for his actions. His response indicates his motivation all along was based more on selfishness—what he could get out of the relationship—which is not biblical love. Men are especially vulnerable to engaging in this kind of behavior.

A FALSE VIEW OF LOVE AND SEX

Unfortunately, in one way or another, this kind of sad story happens all the time. Many young people are confused about love and sex. In fact, have you ever wondered why so many Hollywood movie stars are in and out of so many relationships? And each time they enter a new relationship, they often say, "I'm really in love this time! This is the person for me—forever!"

Guess what? More often than not, the relationship doesn't last. Why? These people are confused as well—just like Bill and Julie. They don't understand true love—as defined in the Bible. And even more unfortunately, these couples are modeling for millions of young people a false view of love and sex.

GOD'S PLAN: SEX IS FOR MARRIAGE

When God created Adam and Eve, they were certainly sexually attracted to each other. God designed them that way. Moses described this relationship as becoming "one flesh" (Genesis 2:24). Both Jesus and the apostle Paul quoted this Old Testament passage when they described the sexual union:

> For this reason a man will leave his father and mother and be *joined to his wife*, and the two will become *one flesh* (Ephesians 5:31, emphasis added; see also Matthew 19:5).

In God's sight, Eve was Adam's *wife*—not his girlfriend or significant other. Thereafter, it was the Lord's divine plan that sexual intimacy is for marriage—a "one man and one woman" relationship for life. In fact, when Jesus quoted Moses, He also said, "So they are no longer two, but *one flesh*. Therefore what God has joined together, *man must not separate*" (Matthew 19:6, emphasis added).

Christlike Love

When Paul instructed husbands to "love" their "wives," just as Christ loved the church, he was describing an act of love that was much more comprehensive than sexual intimacy. In fact, Paul was describing God's love that caused Jesus Christ to give His life for us on the cross and die for our sins. This is our model. As men, we are to love our wives as Christ loved us. This kind of love describes *actions*, not just feelings. In fact, when we practice this kind of love, we do what is right regardless of how we feel.

In chapter 14, we looked carefully at God's definition of love, where Paul actually described this kind of love (see 1 Corinthians 13). Even when we don't have positive feelings, Christlike love . . .

- Is patient when we feel impatient
- Is kind when we want to be unkind
- Is unselfish when we feel jealous
- Is humble when we feel prideful
- Does what is right when we are tempted to do what is wrong
- Puts others first when we want to be first
- Keeps anger from becoming sinful
- Forgives and forgets when we want to hold grudges

This is biblical love that reflects Christ's love for us and is the kind of love that we should have for each other. Again, this kind of love does what is right even if we have feelings that tempt us to do what is wrong and out of the will of God.

Christlike Affection

Making right decisions when we would rather do the opposite does not mean that we cannot and should not enjoy loving feelings that accompany right actions. Paul described this kind of love when he instructed the Christians in Rome to "show *family affection* to one another with *brotherly love*" (Romans 12:10a, emphasis added). Here Paul used a different Greek word to describe these loving feelings. You see, God created us to be able to enjoy loving others in a way that is *non-sexual*. For example, this is the kind of affectionate love I have toward my sisters and my brothers in my family. This is the kind of love I have toward my daughters and my son.

This is the kind of love I have toward my grandsons and granddaughters, and it is also the kind of love I have toward my brothers and sisters in Jesus Christ.

God has recorded some unique biblical examples of this kind of loving affection and friendship. In the Old Testament there was the relationship between David and Jonathan. They loved each other deeply, but certainly in a non-sexual way. In the New Testament, we have the relationship between Jesus and the apostle John. Though Jesus Christ was and is God's Son, He was also "the Son of man." In his humanness, He dearly loved John the apostle more than any of the other disciples. Without showing favoritism, He deeply enjoyed John's friendship.

And let's not forget that this is the kind of love we have observed between Paul and Timothy. Paul loved Timothy as if he were his own son, and Timothy loved Paul as if he were his own father. In these "friendship" relationships, it's also clear that we must never allow feelings of affection to lead to sexual thoughts and actions. However, if you ever discover that these feelings emerge, you need to seek help and advice immediately from a trusted mature Christian adult.

Christlike Sex

We've already noted that God has created us with a capacity to love at the sexual level. In the Old Testament, Solomon described this kind of love in a very specific way. Before he violated God's will by marrying foreign women, he deeply loved one woman, and she loved him. At that time, they had what appears to be an ideal relationship. What he described in the Song of Songs is God's perspective on sexual love. This is a dimension of love that God designed for a marriage between one man and one woman to be enjoyed to the full. However, Solomon allowed his desire for power and illegitimate relationships to lead him out of God's will. Consequently, he paid a horrible price for his sin.

THREE-DIMENSIONAL LOVE

We can illustrate these three dimensions of love visually. Note the figure on the following page. The outer circle represents Christlike love that does what is right and best for someone because it is God's will. We can call this *agapao* love—the Greek word that New Testament writers use the most to describe this kind of love. The next interrelated circle describes positive and affectionate feelings toward others that always act in Christlike ways, never violating God's will. We can call this *phileo* love, a Greek word Paul used to describe love at a non-sexual level (see Romans 12:10).

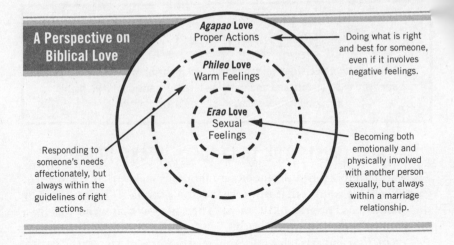

The inner circle involves the most intimate act of love that God designed for husbands and wives. We can call this sexual dimension *erao* love. When we violate the will of God by engaging in a sexual relationship outside the bonds of marriage, we are violating the act of love that always does what is right.

Bill and Julie violated God's will when they engaged in sexual intimacy. When they both had strong feelings of sexual attraction toward each other, they deceived themselves and did what was wrong in God's sight. Because they were not loving each other as Christ loved them, what could have become a God-created capacity for strong physical and emotional attraction became selfish and superficial and eventually turned to resentment.

Unfortunately, in today's world, love is very frequently defined as sexual attraction, as illustrated with the inner circle in the figure. In other words, erotic feelings become the basis for defining love. However, when the realities of life interfere with and distort these strong feelings, people conclude that they no longer love each other. Consequently, they bail out of the relationship. They don't understand that these sexual feelings ebb and flow, and it's Christlike love that sustains a relationship in difficult times (the outer circle in the figure). This is why so many couples "break up" and why so many married people get divorced. The relationship was never based on God's definition of love. Unfortunately, more and more men and women are deceived by the same misunderstanding regarding God's plan for love and sex.

PRINCIPLE TO LIVE BY
THREE-DIMENSIONAL LOVE

To make right decisions regarding your relationship with the opposite sex, you must understand and practice three-dimensional love that is first and foremost based on God's love for you.

GOD TRUSTS YOU TO LEAD . . . START TODAY!

The world paints a very different picture about sexual love than the Word of God. The Bible teaches that true love waits. We shouldn't be surprised by this contrast. As Proverbs 14:12 states, "There is a way that seems right to a man, but its end is the way to death."

Premarital and extramarital sexual relationships often create destructive emotional forces in a marriage relationship that ultimately drive people apart rather than bring them closer together. A sexual relationship within marriage is designed by God to be very fulfilling, but it is often very sensitive and fragile. Even as Christians, a husband and wife must nurture and care for this relationship.

Satan hates healthy marriages because they reflect a relationship with God and they are a witness to the world. It shouldn't surprise us that the enemy of our soul works overtime to accomplish two goals: *to get couples to be sexually active before marriage* and then *create tension and stress within marriage*.

As a young man, God wants you to set the physical boundaries in your relationships with the opposite sex. Never create a situation where your date has to say "no" or "stop" or "far enough!" When we, as men, allow this to happen, we're abdicating our God-given leadership strength and responsibility. We are letting our date or girlfriend lead in the relationship during dating and courtship. So what do you think happens when you get married? There will be conflict. Think about it. If you go through courtship abdicating your leadership role, you will not be in a position to lead *after* you get married. This often leads to confusion, rejection and hurt.

God knew what He was doing when He asked us to "wait" and save our bodies for our spouses after marriage. His paths are perfect, even when we don't understand His plans. Following His plans, of course, can feel very difficult and confusing; but if we exercise our spiritual muscles and follow Him in faith, He will honor us. Remember, you need to train in such a way as to win the race. This training, at times, takes place in the heat of the battle. By fleeing temptation, you are reflecting God's love and grace.

Right now you don't know where the path of life will lead, but He asks you to follow the truths He's given you in the Bible. When you exercise and train your spiritual muscles, you'll be ready to respond like Joseph did when Potiphar's wife tried to seduce him. You will have already made the right decision before you face the temptation.

A PRAYER FOR YOU

Dear God, thank You for loving us and making us whole. We pray for our brothers reading this book, and we pray the same prayer for ourselves. Help us to take the path that is "unnatural." Help us to know and discern between the lies the world teaches and the truths stated in Your Word, the Scriptures. Give us the strength to exercise purity in our relationships and in our free time and when we are using technology. Turn our hearts to You and help us to lean on You and learn what it means to grow as Your child. Protect our hearts and help us to honor the women in our lives. Help our actions and words to encourage them and protect them. Heavenly Father, help us to grow in our relationship with You and to depend on Your strength for righteous living. In Jesus' name. Amen.

God bless you!
Gene and Kenton

ALSO BY
GENE A. GETZ

The Measure of a Man
Twenty Attributes of a Godly Man
ISBN 978.08307.34955

The Measure of a Woman
What *Really* Makes a Woman Beautiful
(with Elaine A. Getz)
ISBN 978.08307.32869

For information on seminars on
The Measure of a Man as well as
The Measure of a Young Man,
contact Gene Getz at 1-800-RENEWAL
or ggetz@renewalradio.org.

Available at Bookstores Everywhere!
Go to **www.regalbooks.com** to learn more about your
favorite Regal books and authors. Visit us online today!

Regal
God's Word for Your World™
www.regalbooks.com